CHART

Egypt Kings	*Babylonia* Kings	*Assyria* Kings
		Shamshi-Adad I 1749-1717
Khyan		
	Samsuditana 1561-1531	
Amenhotep III 1402-1366		
Amenhotep IV 1366-1347 (Akhenaten)		
Tutankhamen 1347-1338		Ashur-uballit I 1336-1330
Horemheb 1334-1307		
		Adad-nirari I 1308-1276
Ramesses II 1290-1223	Kadashman-Turgu 1292-1274	
	Kadashman-Enlil 1274-1268	Shalmaneser I 1276-1246
Merenptah 1223-1209		Tutulti-Ninurta I 1246-1209

HATTUSHA

HATTUSHA

The Capital of the Hittites

KURT BITTEL

New York OXFORD UNIVERSITY PRESS 1970

Library of Congress Catalogue Card Number: 70-83060

Printed in the United States of America

PREFACE

The six lectures which follow were delivered by the author as holder of the Mary Flexner Lectureship at Bryn Mawr College in April and May 1967. All the lectures concern Hattusha, the capital of the Hittite empire, one of the most eminent cities of the ancient Near East, and for some centuries a very important political center. Five of the lectures (i-iv, vi) deal with the history, topography, and monuments of the city; one (v) with the political and cultural relations of the Hittite empire and its capital with Pharaonic Egypt—one of the other great powers of the second millennium B.C. Although we are in possession of some archaeological sources of information, an entirely unclear picture would be conveyed were they not supplemented by a considerable amount of literary evidence.

The printed text is, apart from slight alterations, the same as that of the lectures delivered in 1967. A selected bibliography listing essential publications on the subject of the individual lecture has been provided for each chapter. Diagrams drawn especially for the book will, I hope, contribute to the understanding of the text.

The number of illustrations is approximately that shown to the original audience. That this or that picture has been exchanged for another needs no special justification.

To Dr. Katherine E. McBride, president of Bryn Mawr College, I once again express my thanks for the kind invitation to Bryn Mawr. She, together with other colleagues, made my stay there such an agreeable one that I count it among my most pleasant and unforgettable memories.

I am deeply indebted to Professor Machteld J. Mellink of the Department of Classical and Near Eastern Archaeology. From the day of my arrival in Bryn Mawr to the completion of the printing of this book, which without her unfailing care and great patience could never have been published, she helped me in the kindest way. For this I most warmly thank her.

My thanks also go to Professor Charles Mitchell for his undertaking with unstinting generosity the revision of the English text and for his many valuable suggestions in this connection.

Mrs. Carol W. Carpenter, Curator of Slides and Photographs, Mrs. Tamara S. Wheeler, draftsman, and Miss Louise Alpers, who prepared a clean copy of the manuscript, all contributed substantially to the making of this book and have my sincere gratitude. The greater part of the maps, drawings, and photographs were prepared by Klaus Beck, Barbara Grunewald, Paul Krüger, Rudolf Naumann, Peter Neve, Peter Röhe-Hansen, and Peter Steyer, all active members of the Boğazköy Expedition.

I am most obliged to the editors of the Oxford University Press, who bestowed every possible care on the production of this book.

K. B.

Berlin
December 1969

CONTENTS

Stratigraphic Table ix

I Landscape, Exploration, Archives, Historical Tradition 3

II Hattusha. The City: Historical Development and Monuments 24

III Hattusha. The Royal Fortress of the 14th and 13th Centuries B.C. 63

IV Yazılıkaya 91

V The Hittite Empire and Egypt in the Light of the Excavations and Archives of Boğazköy 113

VI Hattusha-Boğazköy in Phrygian and Persian Times 132

Bibliography 159

Index 171

STRATIGRAPHIC TABLE

Correlation of Levels and Periods of Hattusha

Historical Periods	*Büyükkale*	*Area of the "House on the Slope"*	*Lower Terrace*	*Main Periods of the City*
Pre-Hittite	f e d V c	9 8c-8d	5	Transition from the Early to the Middle Bronze Age (1)
	b a	8b		Pre-Hittite Hattush (2)
Assyrian merchant colonies (later phase)	IV d	8a	4	
Old Hittite Period	IV c 3 IV c 2 IV c 1	7	3	[Before 1700 B.C.] Hattusha, Capital of the Old Kingdom (3)
Hittite Empire	IV b IV a III b III a	6 5	2 1b 1a	Capital of the Hittite Empire (4) [±1200 B.C.]
Post-Hittite/ Phrygian	II	4 3		Iron Age Settlement Pteria (?)
Phrygian	I a I b	2		
	Scanty Hellenistic and Roman Occupation	1		

Table showing the layers of the different centers of the old city. —— = destruction layer.

HATTUSHA

I

LANDSCAPE, EXPLORATION, ARCHIVES, HISTORICAL TRADITION

In 1957 the excavations at Boğazköy, about a hundred miles east of Ankara in Anatolia, yielded a cuneiform text which in two languages, Hittite and Akkadian, describes a very interesting event (plate 1). We read about the Great King Hattushili I, an energetic ruler and military leader who reigned about or shortly before 1600 B.C.: "In those days he set forth. Like a lion the Great King crossed the river Puran. The city of Hashshu(wa) he overwhelmed like a lion with his paw. Dust he poured on it and with its possessions he filled Hattusha. Silver and gold knew neither beginning nor end. The Weather God, Lord of Armaruk, the Weather God, Lord of Halap, Allatum, Adalur and Liluri, two bulls of silver, three statues of silver and gold, two hamri-buildings. . . . I had framed in gold and the door likewise I had framed in gold. One table—good gold— . . . , three tables of silver, one golden throne with armrests—good gold— . . .

Figure 1. Map of Anatolia and Syria showing sites referred to in text

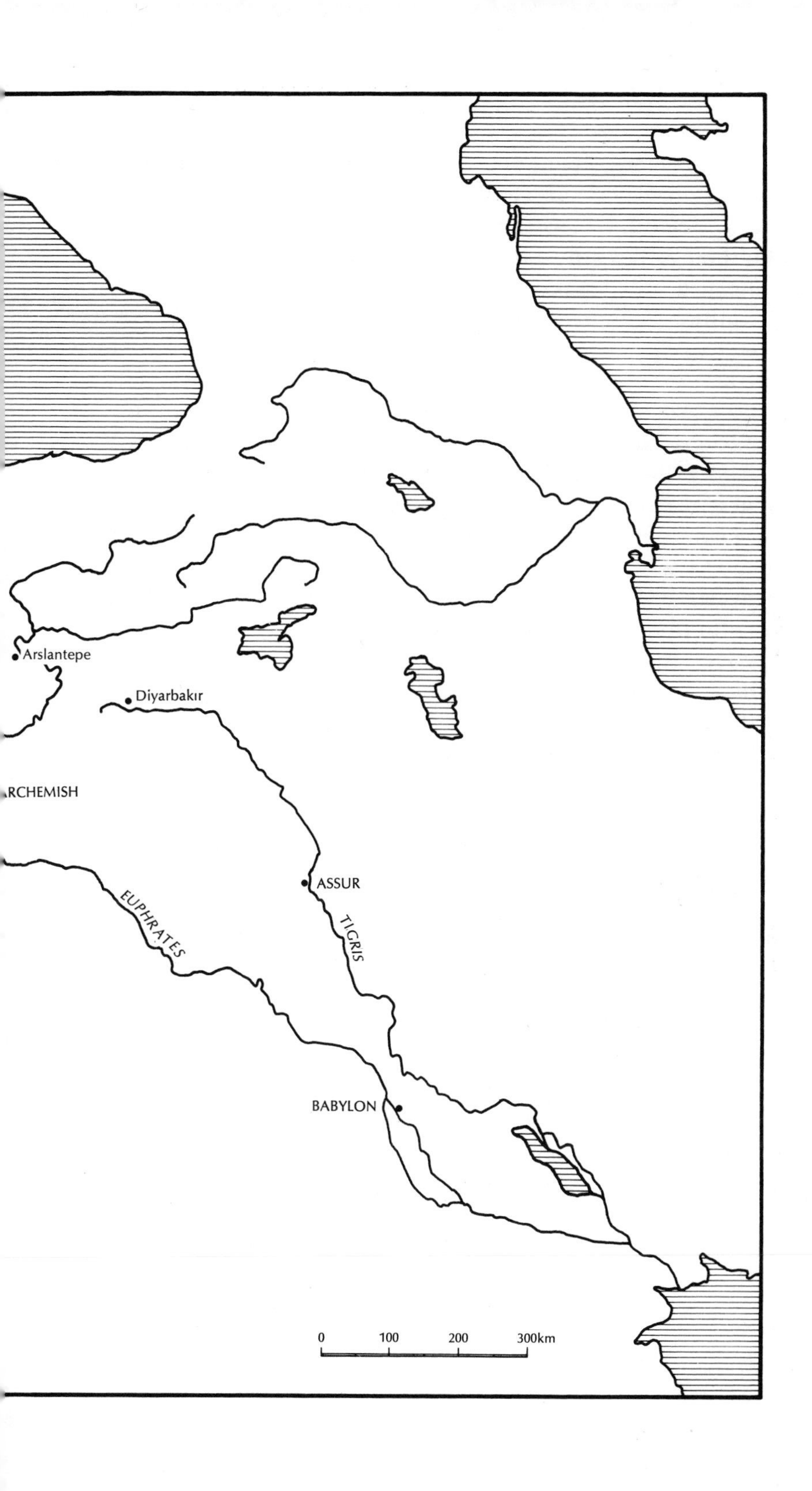

Arslantepe
Diyarbakır
RCHEMISH
ASSUR
TIGRIS
EUPHRATES
BABYLON
0
100
200
300km

set with precious stones and gold, all of these . . . I took from Hashshu up to the Sun Goddess of Arinna. The daughter of the goddess Allatum, Hepat, three statues of silver, two statues of gold, those I took up to the temple of the goddess Mezulla. . . ."

The text still speaks clearly to us today. The king has been on a military campaign, one among many, as we know. He has crossed a river called Puran (Puruna in another version), which must be near the upper Euphrates. He has captured the city of Hashshu, where he collected rich booty: statues and equipment of precious metal, partly encrusted with precious stones. With this booty "he filled Hattusha," taking part of it up to the Sun Goddess of Arinna, part to the temple of the goddess Mezulla. The expression "up" seems to imply that the temples of these two goddesses were located in an upper part of the city of Hattusha, as if one had to ascend to them. We shall have to look into this later on. Hattusha reappears in this text a number of times. In the twentieth section, after a brief survey of the events of a particular year, we read: "then I came home to Hattusha." This means that this city is the king's residence and the seat of his government. The entire text in which the king himself addresses us is prefaced by this sentence: "The Great King Tabarna exercised his royal rule in Hattusha, Tawananna's brother's son." Tabarna is a title due to the Great Kings; the second phrase means that the king is indeed a member of the royal dynasty, but instead of being the son of his predecessor he is a nephew of the queen. This does not concern us at the moment. What counts is first that Hattusha about 1600 B.C. was the capital of a ruling Hittite Great King; secondly, that this city boasted several temples of deities to whom the king offered the booty from his military campaigns as votive gifts, evidently as a token of thanks for their support during the battles; and thirdly, that this Great King Hattushili, "the man from Hattusha," even in his name professes his ties to that city. Although this is not our oldest extant reference to Hattusha, it is the earliest to attest its status as the Hittite capital.

Where was this Hattusha, what do we know about it, and what, above all, are the sources of our knowledge?

In 1905 an Assyriologist from Berlin, Hugo Winckler, went to Boğazköy, a small Turkish village east of the middle course of the Halys river, the Kızıl Irmak, in Northern Cappadocia (plates 2, 3a). This was the site of extensive ruins, discovered by the Frenchman Charles Texier in 1834 and made known by him in a volume of plates which created a stir among historians and archaeologists in Europe. The size of the ruins and the debris of several monumental buildings soon made it clear that these were the remains of an important city-site, not a simple settlement. Ancient sources suggested an identification either with Tavium, the center of the Trocmian tribe of the Galatians, or with Pteria, a Cappadocian city mentioned by Herodotus as captured and destroyed by the Lydian king Croesus in 547 B.C. during his campaign into Median territory across the Halys. In favor of the first identification seemed to be Strabo's report (XII. 567) that Tavium had a temple of Zeus with a colossal bronze statue of the god in a sacred precinct with an asylum; and indeed among the ruins of Boğazköy there was a monumental complex built of huge masonry which could have been the temple of Ζεὺς Ταουιανός, Jupiter Tavianus. But those who identified the place with Herodotus' Pteria drew attention to the extremely archaic character of the walls of the buildings, to their unclassical appearance, and especially to several sculptures in the city and rock reliefs near it which seemed reminiscent of Assyrian, or as other experts had it, of Iranian-Sacian art. These sculptures definitely suggested not a Graeco-Roman but an Asiatic artistic tradition, and hardly suited Hellenistic-Imperial Tavium.

Then in 1884 Sitlington-Sterrett traveled in the area for the Archaeological Institute of America and proved epigraphically that Tavium lay near the modern village of Büyük Nefes, eleven miles to the southwest of Boğazköy. This eliminated Tavium. And even the probability that Boğazköy might have been Pteria, at least so far as its origin and *floruit* were concerned, gradually dwindled. W. Wright in 1884 led the way to the right solution. Soon afterwards A. H. Sayce recognized the true context of the sculptures in question. He saw that they and many other sculptures formed a stylistic group linked with a peculiar pictographic script. This group belonged to a culture which reached, as it was thought at the time, from Hama in the valley of the Syrian Orontes to the Sipylos mountain far to the west in the hinterland of Smyrna. Sayce called this culture Hittite, after the Kheta of the Egyptians, the Hittim of the Old Testament, the real center of whose power and culture was thought to be in Northern Syria. Boğazköy and its ruins would have been merely at the edge of this cultural area, and the prevailing opinion at the beginning of this century was that Boğazköy unquestionably had once been an important city, but still no more than the capital of a dynasty of limited power whose authority would not have extended beyond the borders of Cappadocia.

In 1894 the Frenchman Ernest Chantre and the German E. Schäffer found some fragments of cuneiform tablets of baked clay in the ruins. Their discovery in this part of Asia Minor came as a surprise, but they seemed to support Sayce's early date for the site and its presumed dependence on a cultural focus in Syria. Some of these texts were written in a language which was then not understood, but is now called "Hittite" or "cuneiform Hittite" or "Neshite," an Indo-European idiom. The remainder of the texts, however, turned out to be in the so-called Akkadian language, and appeared to be contemporary with the famous Amarna tablets, found in 1887, which belonged to the first half of the 14th century B.C., the period of the pharaohs Amenhotep III and Amenhotep IV. Among the Amarna tablets there were some records of the Hittite king Shuppiluliuma and two letters in a special language to and from the king of Arzawa, a land in Asia Minor. Since many tablet fragments found at Boğazköy revealed the same language as the Arzawa letter from Amarna, Boğazköy began to be considered the capital of Arzawa. When Hugo Winckler, to whom we now return, traveled to Boğazköy in 1905, he too thought that he might find the capital of Arzawa, a genuine Anatolian state of the 14th century B.C. and a minor power in the ancient world of that era.

In 1906 Winckler and Theodore Makridi started extensive excavations in the ruins of Boğazköy; tablets were found that summer on the west slope of a hill called Büyükkale, which will be prominent in our later discussions. There were about 2,500 of them; they were diverse in content; they were mostly in fragments; and they once formed part of a royal archives or library. So far as they were written in Akkadian, they were readily understandable. They comprised letters and treaties, testimonies of the diplomatic contacts among the courts of those days and their mutual agreements. Several of the letters belonged to the correspondence between the kings of Egypt and Hatti, Ramesses II and Hattushili (Hattushili III, as he is now known). Then on August 20, 1906, Winckler and Makridi found the Akkadian version of a treaty already known in essentials from an Egyptian hieroglyphic text carved on the temple walls of Karnak near Thebes in Upper Egypt. This was the treaty concluded in the twenty-first year of Ramesses II, 1270 B.C., with Hattushili III, the Lugal-GAL, the Great King of the Hittite Empire. These letters and treaties between the great powers could not possibly have belonged to the archives of a court like Arzawa. They furnished definite proof that the true center of the Hittite Empire was not in Northern Syria but was here in the heart of Asia Minor, at the ruined city near Boğazköy. Its name now turned out to be "the city of Hatti," Hattusha. In those days Winckler reconstructed from the available records a dynasty of seven kings spanning five generations, *c.* 1400-1200 B.C. He could not suspect that future research would prove that there was a much longer dynasty, nor on the basis of the then limited knowledge of Anatolian toponymy could he know that the name of the city was originally not Hittite, but in its older form "Hattush" stemmed from pre-Hittite times.

Since the days of Hugo Winckler's great discoveries, the excavation of the ruins of Boğazköy has been continued systematically. Winckler worked with Makridi in 1907, 1911, and 1912; in 1907 jointly with a second expedition under Otto Puchstein which investigated the fortifications and five monumental buildings, three or four of which were identified as temples. As early as 1883 Carl Humann had made a plan of the city on the basis of the preserved and restorable evidence, but we owe to Puchstein's expedition our first real knowledge of the range and the size of the city, of the city-wall in its main circuit, and of the character of Anatolian Hittite architecture in a number of outstanding examples. Then the Balkan War, the First World War, the Graeco-Turkish War and the resulting unstable conditions in Anatolia interrupted the work for many years. Not until 1931 were the excavations resumed, this time under the joint auspices of the German Archaeological Institute and the German Orient Society. Annual campaigns followed until the outbreak of World War II, which caused a second major interruption until 1951.

From 1952 until the present, Boğazköy-Hattusha has been under excavation on a larger or smaller scale in annual summer and fall campaigns. All told, twenty-eight campaigns have been devoted to the investigation of the ruins of Boğazköy. Some of these campaigns were restricted in time and scope, but altogether a great deal of time has been spent on the recovery of Hattusha. Even so, no more than part of this unusually vast city can be called explored, and large districts in the city area have not yet been touched at all. They may, and in many places undoubtedly do, contain important evidence. Many questions about the ancient city have still not been answered, but one may hope that at least partial answers will be reached in the future.

We have seen that the nucleus of the Hittite Empire (Hatti) was at one time thought to have been in North Syria. After Winckler's proof that Boğazköy, far to the north, was the capital of this empire, scholars recognized that central Asia Minor should not be seen as the fringe but as the heart of the empire. Further research proved that Central Anatolia was the crucial area, where in pre-Empire days Hatti had developed its supremacy over many rival principalities. But all this, and the rise of Hatti as a great power in the course of the late 15th and early 14th centuries, has long since become an established part of our knowledge of Western Asiatic history of the second millennium B.C., and so need not detain us here. We must, however, briefly consider the geographical situation of the capital.

The maps reveal (figs. 1, 2) that at the time of the greatest expansion of the Hittite Empire—an expansion which went principally in the direction of the ancient centers of culture in the southeast and south, in North Mesopotamia and Syria—the capital did lie in a peripheral northern position rather than a central one. However, Hattusha remained the capital, as we will see, throughout its long history except for one brief episode.

It seems that Hittite conservatism made the royal court and the nobles of the realm, including the priesthood, cling to the old 17th-century capital. This conservative tendency betrays itself in many other aspects of life in Hatti, not only in matters of government. The marginal position of Hattusha, however, becomes even more curious when we realize that the northern boundary of the empire, never really fixed and always in some state of flux, was on the average less than thirty miles distant from the capital. And beyond this border lived the highly aggressive Kashka people, who were basically never pacified and internally not even organized in the political sense. From the 15th century or earlier, until the end of the 13th century B.C. they again and again invaded Hittite territory in spite of all Hittite countermeasures. In the area of the upper Halys they repeatedly penetrated far to the south and at least once succeeded in capturing Hattusha itself, causing heavy destruction. This happened during a period of serious political and military weakness of the empire, yet the court and government did not want to sever connections with the old metropolis. But this is not all: in its geographical setting Hattusha is much more oriented to the north than to the south. Solid mountain formations separate it from the plains of Cappadocia, from the Taurus passes in the south, from the steppes of Tyana directly north of the Taurus, from the fertile basin of Kayseri-Caesarea at the foot of the enormous Mons Argaeus, and from the vast Central Anatolian plateau and

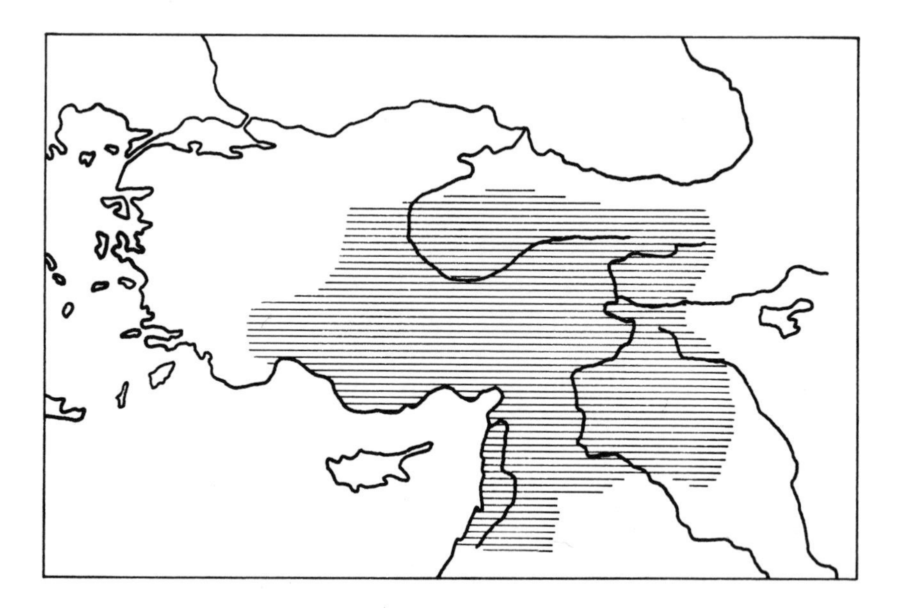

Figure 2. Sketch map showing the extent of the Hittite Empire

the reaches of the Great Salt Lake. These mountains rise to some 6,000 feet in Kapaktepe directly to the south of Hattusha. They do not cut off all contact, but they lie like a barrier between the capital and the heart of Anatolia, where natural lines of communication radiate to the southeast, south, and west. The basic domain of the capital is a valley some twenty-five miles long, with extensions to the northwest and northeast, formed by a small river which further down joins the Delice Irmak, probably the ancient Cappadox flumen. This in turn is an eastern tributary of the Halys, the great river which flows into the Black Sea. All these topographical and hydrographic factors point to the north, away from the center of Anatolia.

Nowadays there is little vegetation near the city, except in isolated patches. The stony ground is cultivated as much as possible but the total effect is meager and sparse in a thinly populated area. Natural clusters of trees or true forests are lacking altogether. This has not always been the case. Not too long ago there was much woodland. From Carl Humann's description we gather that some eighty years ago large areas within the ancient city were still covered with oak scrub. Shortly before that, huge oaks still grew in the southern part of the city. All of that is gone nowadays. But some hills to the west and south still have isolated thickets, the last remnants of more solid forests of the past. Such forests must have been considerable in the Hittite era, since timber played a prominent role in Anatolian-Hittite architecture, not only in simple private buildings but in all types of monumental construction. Enormous quantities of timber were used, as we shall see later on, and could not possibly have been transported *in toto* from a remote source of supply. The capital itself must have been surrounded by a wealth of forest and timber. The selection of this site for the capital and its durability may be partly due to this ample supply of timber combined with the presence of water. Water here is abundant by Anatolian standards, with no fewer than seven springs in the city area.

In two instances wooden beams were so well preserved in Hittite buildings that their species could be determined. In a 14th-century building the timber turned out to be deciduous oak, in one of the 13th century, pine. A passage from a ritual text found in one of the local archives may be relevant in this context: "In the morning a decorated carriage stands ready in front of the temple; three ribbons, one red, one white, one blue, are tied to it. They harness the chariot and bring out the god from the temple and seat him in the carriage." Several women go in front, holding lighted torches ". . . and the god comes behind, and they take the god down through the Tawinian gate to the wood."

This is a ceremony in which the cult statue of a god is taken from his temple and driven in a chariot out of the city to a forest where, as the text continues, the statue is cleansed—or rather, bathed—in a brook. This of course is a procedure known from many ancient cults. The Tawinian gate, which gives us a topographical clue to the proceedings, is one of the northern city-gates of Hattusha. It is named after the first city along the road

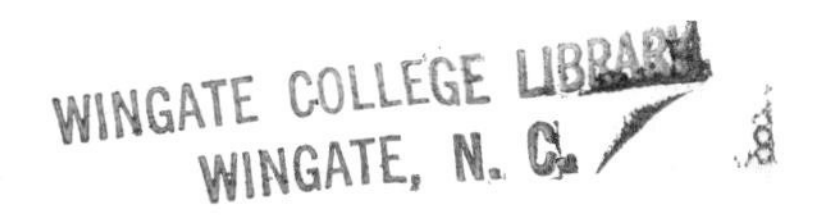

from the capital to the north. This gate is situated in the lowest part of the city area, hence the wording of the text: "and they take the god down through the Tawinian gate . . ."; the point of departure is one of the temples on much higher ground, to be discussed later. In front of the Tawinian gate there must have been a forest which has now vanished. We have quoted this Hittite text from the local archives in some detail because it clearly proves that the landscape in the immediate vicinity of Hattusha was essentially different from what we see now. We can take it for granted that there were many other forests near the capital, but only one happens to be mentioned in the preserved texts.

Several times we have had occasion to mention or quote passages from the Hittite archives or libraries which were discovered in the excavations; and we shall have to deal with a considerable number of these documents in the course of these chapters. It seems appropriate, therefore, to offer some basic comments at this stage. The Hittites acquired the art of writing in the early second millennium B.C. They took the so-called cuneiform script from the Babylonians, probably by way of North Syria, and developed a scribal tradition of their own comparatively soon. This goes for their own language, Hittite, as well as for the Babylonian tongue, so-called Akkadian. They used tablets of clay on which the signs were impressed with a stylus, but they also engraved the signs on metal tablets or applied them to wooden tablets with a brush. All the documents of the second and third category have perished, and we know of their existence only from occasional references. The office, for instance, of the "scribe of the wooden tablets" is very well known though no single product of this kind of Hittite writing has been preserved. Favorable conditions of preservation, e.g. in very humid soil, might still reveal one. But 22,000 cuneiform clay tablets, though mostly fragmentary, have so far been found in the excavations of Boğazköy. They were once collected and arranged in proper archives. Three archives, two large and one smaller, were discovered within the palace of the Great King, and another one in a building which was part of the greatest temple of the city, the temple of the Weather God of Hatti. As for the contents of these archives, there is no proof of a basic difference between those of the palace and that of the temple. All kinds of texts that make up Hittite literature are found in both places. There are, nevertheless, some exceptions. Treaties concluded with vassal states or foreign powers were found mostly in the archive of the great temple. The parties swore to observe the regulations of the treaties while invoking the great deities of the state. Hence these treaties were deposited in the sacred precinct so that the gods might watch over their observance. But here too there are exceptions. The most famous of all Hittite treaties, concluded, as mentioned above, between Ramesses II of Egypt and Hattushili III, was not deposited in the temple archive but in the royal palace. Permanently, one wonders, or just temporarily and caught in the destruction? The letters exchanged with civil and military servants in the provinces (of which unfortunately there are very few left) or with the dynasts of foreign courts, were mostly found in the archives of the royal palace. They clearly had to be at hand in the state chancellery for reference in day-to-day correspondence. Obviously, we found not only the incoming letters but also copies of those dispatched by order of the king. Out of an excavated total of fifty-one letters between Ramesses II and Queen Naptera of Egypt on the one hand, and Hattushili III and his Queen Puduhepa on the other, only four were discovered in the temple archives, against forty-six in the archives of the palace.

What did such an archive look like, how was it arranged, and how did it function? It is obvious that in a city which suffered violent destruction and pillage, whatever survives of the archive buildings is in ruinous condition. But a careful system of excavation whereby even the smallest fragments were noted and their findspots entered on the plan, made it possible to reconstruct an archive room in the palace in its essential features (plate 3b). The walls, built of sun-dried mudbrick and a considerable amount of wood, were destroyed by fire and turned into a hard, brick-like substance. Nevertheless, it was still evident that low benches had once existed on the floors against the base of the walls. Partly on these mud-plastered stone benches, and partly scattered over the floor of the archive room, a great many clay tablets were found, most of them broken. The debris overlying the floor contained a great deal of burned wood near the benches, indications that the tablets once stood on wooden shelves like our books today. The shelves were set up along the walls, the stone benches serving as their bases. In the great fire which destroyed the archive, the shelves collapsed and the tablets fell to the floor, most of them breaking to pieces. Close observation of the findspots, however, allowed us not only to restore some almost complete large tablets out of the fragments but also, though in regrettably few instances, to ascertain in what order approximately the tablets had once been arranged on the shelves. There was, incidentally, no systematic order according to contents, but this lack of systematization may not always have prevailed in the archives of the Hittite capital. Quite possibly the collections of clay tablets have come down to us not in their original order but in a rearrangement which Great King Tuthaliya IV (around 1250-1220 B.C.) was forced to make due to circumstances to be described below. This may account for the loss of a great many texts.

The clay tablets were written by scribes of whom many are known to us by name, since they signed the texts they wrote. We know that there were generations of scribes, in which this highly respected Hittite office was transmitted from father to son. There were schools for scribes, since a few tablets show by their contents and ductus that they were exercises by beginners in the art of writing. The Dub.Sar, the scribe of clay tablets, also had to look after the arrangement and administration of the archives. Small tablets of clay on which a text or a series of texts was indicated by only a catchword probably served as labels. They occur in all the archives of the Hittite capital, though by no means as frequently as might be expected. Many must be lost. Presumably they were set so their captions were visible and readable on the shelves where the relevant tablets stood. There are also tablets inscribed with very brief summaries of the texts which were, or should be, available; these were obviously catalogues of holdings. For us they are of great value not only because they give an idea of the way the archives were ordered and supervised, but also because they list many works which have not survived but whose titles we learn in this manner. The happiest hours of an excavation are when, as in 1957 in Boğazköy-Hattusha, such an archive is exposed and a catalogue is found whose entries are partly preserved in the very same room. Who could fail to appreciate such direct and personal contact with an institution of the distant past, through millennia?

Numerous though the documents found in the archives may be, the number of those relevant to the history or, for that matter, the topography of the Hittite capital is deplorably meager. An additional difficulty is that Hattusha often does not mean the town but the country. When this is clearly indicated, as in an Old Hittite text saying "he reigned in the land of Hattusha," no problem exists. Where, however, it says merely "Hattusha" or "Hatti" without any qualification, the name can only be related to the capital if this is self-evident from the context. This is not so in the literary text with the oldest known reference to Hatti. It tells among other things that seventeen kings went to war against Naram-Sin, the great ruler of Akkad (23rd century B.C.). Among them were Zipani, king of Kanesh, and Pamba, king of Hatti, both Anatolian dynasts, Kanesh being identical with the mound of Kültepe near Kayseri. It used to be thought that this inscription was partly fictitious and that at the Old Hittite court Anatolian place-names and persons had been inserted in an Old Babylonian literary work in order to lend it a local coloring. But now we know that Sargon of Akkad and his crossing of the Euphrates are referred to in the great document of Hattushili I which was quoted at the beginning of this chapter. This means that the 600-year-old deeds of the kings of Akkad were still remembered by the Old Hittite kings and lived on in their tradition. The judgment on the credibility of the Pamba text will therefore have to be somewhat modified. Certainly the document of Hattushili with the reference to Sargon ranks among the texts which can be regarded as annals, while the other, a literary work, may have been composed with more license. But the fact that one of the texts has proved to be reliable should dissuade us from downright repudiation of the other account. Whether we may consider this Pamba of Hatti to be a king who actually resided in Boğazköy itself at the time of Naram-Sin remains uncertain, whatever one's views of the text as such may be.

For the 19th and 18th centuries B.C., on the other hand, the existence of the town is safely documented. Its name was then Hattush and it was of some importance to the commercial activities of the Old Assyrian merchants whose trading center was at Kanesh, the Kültepe of today in Central Cappadocia. Among the known trading settlements, the colony of Hattush played only a minor part, although considerable transactions were carried out in various directions, especially to and from Kanesh. The Old Assyrian trading records excavated in Boğazköy-Hattusha testify to the presence and activity of Assyrian traders. That the town was a kārum or the seat of a kārum, that is to say a formal trading colony with appropriate officials, seems to be implied by a text in the museum of Kayseri. Its contents have been known for a long time but so far Boğazköy has failed to yield references to a kārum Hattush.

Beside the Assyrian trading establishment there was in the same location also a settlement of native Anatolian—we may call them Hattian—inhabitants, the subjects of a dynasty residing in Hattush. The last ruler of this dynasty is known thanks to a cuneiform document which has come down to us in several copies written in Hittite. This text was incorporated in the archives of the later Hittite capital. It was copied repeatedly and carefully handed down to posterity, because it describes the deeds of a king and conqueror who originally resided in Kushshar, a city not yet located. This Kushshar is, however, the city to which also the later Hittite Great Kings traced their origin. In the famous text of king Anitta of Kushshar the city is not only mentioned but for the first time appears in connection with a specific event. We read:

for the second time came again Pijushti,
king of Hatti,
and whom he brought of his helpers, those
at the town of Salampa I defeated.

And further down:

And hunger plagued the city of Hattusha;
so I let it be. But when it was at last gravely afflicted
with hunger, Shiushmi surrendered it to
the god Halmashuitta; and during the night
I took it by assault. But in its place
I sowed weeds.
Him who will be king after me and
plant Hattusha again
the Weather God of Heaven shall hit!

Anitta, Lord of Kushshar, King of Nesha, is an important figure known to us from documents from Alişar and Kültepe and also from his inscribed dagger found in Kanesh some years ago. He was a prince who achieved a sort of supremacy over other kings of city-states of Central Anatolia and established the first kingdom of considerable authority and size in that area. Among his conquests was the city which now appears under its Hittite name Hattusha and no longer as the pre-Hittite Hattush. It is called Hattusha, too, in a letter written in the time of Zimrilim, found in the archives of Mari on the middle Euphrates.

Anitta destroyed the city and invoked the curse of the Weather God of Heaven on anyone who should try to settle it again. And yet, the city was resettled! This happened, at a conservative estimate, at most a hundred years later and by a king who like the destroyer Anitta traced his dynasty back to the very same city of Kushshar, which in the initial period of his reign was certainly one of his residences. This was King Hattushili I. In one of his great documents he said of himself: "Hattushili, the Great King, King of Hattusha, the man from Kushshar." Kushshar was still his personal residence but Hattusha was the administrative capital. But after him the Hittite kings kept court and resided in Boğazköy-Hattusha. Murshili I, the immediate successor of Hattushili I, actually "reigned in Hattusha."

For the 400 years of history of Hattusha as the capital of the Hittite Empire we learn of only three events from the records in the archives, and even those are not unambiguous. In a probably authentic personal report King Hantili claims to have fortified Hattusha which "was in no way protected by walls before." This would mean that the fortifications were erected shortly after the middle of the 16th century; that they were actually the first ones is open to doubt in spite of Hantili's claim.

Some 150 years later, under the reign of the Great King Tuthaliya III, *c.* 1400 B.C., the city suffered a great catastrophe. A number of hostile hordes, among them the Pontic Kashka, invaded Hatti-land. "And Hattusha, the city, was burnt down, and only . . . and the hesti-house of . . . remained." What exactly is meant by hesti-house is not known. It has something to do with offerings and the cult of the dead and is often mentioned in connection with mausolea. In any case it was spared, perhaps because it lay outside the city, while the city itself went up in flames. But the city must have been rebuilt very soon, at least in its essential parts, since under the reign of the next king, Shuppiluliuma I, it is on record as existing and fully operative.

While the event just referred to occurred as the result of outside interference, the next event which is authenticated by the Hittite archives was due to the initiative of the Hittite court and the Hittite executive power. Hattushili III says of his brother Muwatalli who reigned from 1305 to 1282:

> Thereafter he moved the gods of Hatti and the *Manes* away
> and took them down to Dattashsha and
> made Dattashsha his abode.

And in another passage:

> My brother took up the Hatti-gods,
> the gods of Arinna
> and the . . . gods and took them
> to Dattashsha and made Dattashsha the residence
> and sheltered the gods there . . .
> And the place which
> my brother Muwatalli had required for
> the court, Dattashsha . . .

Thus the Great King Muwatalli moved the capital to a site which we cannot pinpoint exactly, although other references show that it definitely lay in what was then called the "Lower Land." This suggests an area in or south of the Taurus Mountains. From a prayer of the same King Muwatalli we learn that the new residence was in fact in Kummanni, in the region of ancient Comana in Cataonia. This recently found prayer also explains why the capital had to be transferred so far to the southeast: Hattusha had been lost, certainly to enemies from without. Once again hostile hordes, especially the Kashka people again, had invaded from the Pontic Mountains. It was not because he wanted to be nearer to Syria, at that time the principal scene of foreign entanglements, nor because he considered it easier to cope with an imminent military struggle with Egypt from a southern residence, that Muwatalli gave up the traditional capital. These used to be considered the main reasons, but now we know that he was worried by the exposed situation of the capital on the northern periphery of the empire. Northern barbaric tribes overwhelmed it twice within barely a hundred years. Thanks to the discovery of Muwatalli's prayer we can also make better sense now of a passage in a text of his brother Hattushili who later became King Hattushili III. He says of himself, while still the crown prince:

> and then I met the enemy at Hahhas
> and gave him battle. And Ishtar, my
> mistress, helped me
> and I conquered him. And his forces

> I led away.
> But those he had with him from the great city of
> Hattusha:
> I took away from him and let them all live in their
> former places. . . . And that was
> my first deed as a man.

Although the young prince, the brother of the reigning king, had saved the old capital, resettled its inhabitants, and beaten the enemy, Muwatalli did not return to Hattusha, but made Dattashsha his permanent residence. He apparently regarded this transfer as binding for the future, since the gods (i.e. their statues) and the spirits of the dead, the *manes* of the deceased ancestors, were moved from the old to the new residence. One cannot help wondering what condition the city was in after the court had left and the administration had gone elsewhere with all its official institutions, including presumably the state archives. We shall come back to this briefly in a later chapter.

Muwatalli's renunciation of the old capital did not last for very long. His son, Great King Murshili III—as he was called when he ascended the throne, his real name being Urhi-Teshub—restored Hattusha's position as the hereditary capital: "Urhi-Teshub took the gods from Dattashsha up and returned them to Hattusha." He could do so more freely since Hattushili had succeeded in securing the northern frontier of the empire. Thus the threat to the capital seemed to be removed forever. Hattusha's loss of prestige was, therefore, confined to an episode of not more than fifteen or twenty years. Thereafter it continues to be the capital and the seat of the court until the downfall of the empire around 1200 B.C. Documents referring to the last seventy to eighty years of the city itself are lacking.

Historical records of the city and its internal events are then disproportionately scanty. The Hittites contributed much to the development of historiography and the Great Kings left the oldest preserved examples of annalistic reports, some of them 300 years older than the earliest Assyrian ones, but they had remarkably little interest in the recording and transmission of their local history. What little information we have of the history of the city of Hattusha serves merely as the frame of a picture to which only archaeology can lend contours and color. To this we shall turn in the next chapter.

II

HATTUSHA. THE CITY: HISTORICAL DEVELOPMENT AND MONUMENTS

The cuneiform documents found in the archives of Hattusha yield very little direct evidence for the history of the Hittite capital. This is mainly because these documents deal with very different topics, and throw only an occasional and indirect light upon the life of the capital. Furthermore, the Hittites, unlike certain other peoples of the ancient East, had not developed much interest in topography and local history. And unlike the Babylonians and Assyrians, they did not inscribe on a public building details about its purpose, its builder, and the time and occasion of its erection. Whatever Hittite records of this kind have come down to us merely give names of kings, as we shall see later; and since such records were not found *in situ* and are fragmentary, it is still open to doubt whether they originally belonged to specific buildings.

Another type of documentation which was in use in Mesopotamia from Sumerian times and which supplies scholars with an invaluable source of information is totally absent in Hittite civilization. I refer to the tablets which form part of foundation deposits inserted in special locations under buildings. Owing to the verbosity of the Babylonian kings, the text of their foundation tablets is often almost as informative as that of the building inscriptions proper. It is true that the Hittites, too, knew the custom of depositing foundation offerings and were conscious of the magic effect of such provisions. This is evident from building rituals which mention the fact that perishable and imperishable votive objects were placed under the foundations—these ranging from offerings of fruit and miniature tools to offerings of bronze statuettes of gods and winged bulls. One of these texts tells of copper as a foundation offering: "Just as the copper is safe and as it is moreover solid, let this temple be safe, let it stand solidly on the dark earth." It is obvious that these words express the same sort of belief in magic as existed in ancient Mesopotamia. There is, of course, as noted above, a difference in that the Hittite offerings lack the foundation tablets and are primarily silent witnesses yielding no comment on the building itself.

Lacking literary sources of the type which in the ancient center of the Near East are so copious even for the history of individual towns, we must—for the Hittite capital—rely more than ever on strictly archaeological sources, that is, the results provided by excavation. Even here a caveat is in order. The city at the time of its greatest expansion, in the 13th century B.C., measured 414 acres. It was, therefore, much smaller than the Babylon of Nebuchadnezzar or, for that matter, the Nineveh of Sargon II. However, Hattusha enters a special class, for example, when we contrast its 414 acres with the 131 acres occupied by Assur in the 12th century B.C. Viewed in the context of its own age, the area of the city of Hattusha is very large indeed. This alone proves that it was a community of major importance. The excavations so far have revealed only some aspects of this metropolis,

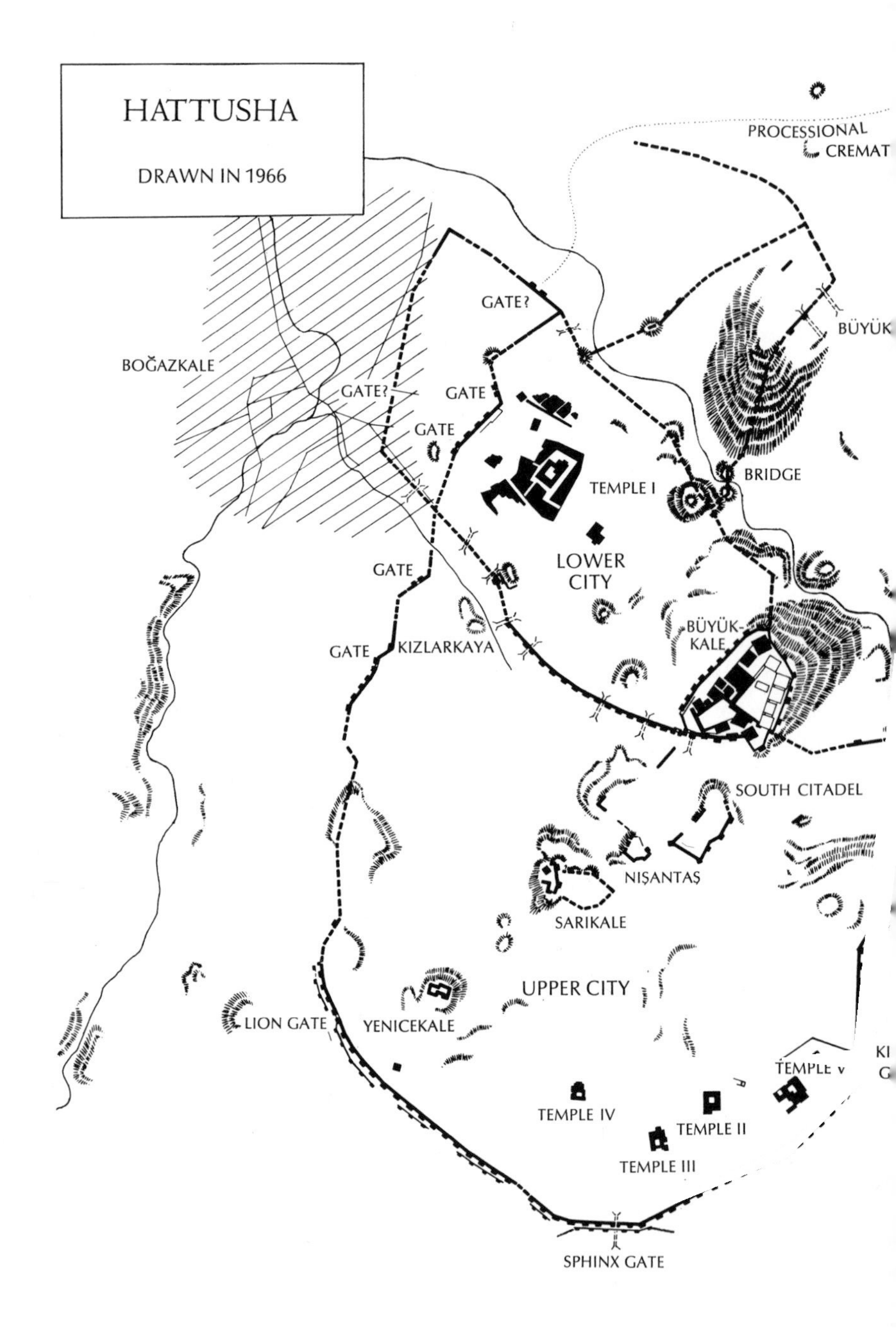

Figure 3. Plan of the city area of Hattusha

YAZILIKAYA?

YAZILIKAYA

N

KAYALIBOĞAZ

0 100 200 300 400 500 600m

though I fancy they are the important ones. Vast sections of the center, however, have not yet been touched and may have major surprises in store for us.

From the size alone of the city area in the 13th century B.C., during the period immediately preceding the fall of Hattusha, we could conclude that this township had grown slowly in several stages from modest beginnings (fig. 3). This has been corroborated by the excavations, which, in their present state, have revealed four principal phases of the history of Boğazköy (plate 4):

1. Small settlements of the latest phase of the Early Bronze Age and of the transition from Early to Middle Bronze Age.
2. Pre-Hittite Hattush of the 19th and 18th centuries B.C. and the Old Assyrian trade establishment (so-called kārum Hattush).
3. Hattusha as the capital of the Old Hittite Kingdom in the 16th and 15th centuries B.C.
4. The capital of the Hittite Empire in the 14th and 13th centuries B.C.

The first and oldest settlement was not founded in virgin territory. Habitation sites which date back at least to the second phase of the Early Bronze Age have been traced in the valley north of Boğazköy (fig. 4). They have also been traced in the seemingly inhospitable mountainous country south of Boğazköy. A site near Cıradere, four miles to the southeast, belongs to the Central Anatolian Early Bronze Age II and III periods and may even go back to Chalcolithic times. There are finds of the Early Bronze Age II period also from and near Büyükkaya, very close to Boğazköy and from Ballıkkaya directly to the north of Yazılıkaya. Hitherto none of these settlements has been closely investigated and we know them only from stray finds. However, in the autumn of 1966, in a trial excavation at Ballıkkaya, we discovered at a slight depth beneath the surface the foundations of a one-room house of the Early Bronze Age and found this settlement of the third millennium to be comparatively well preserved. The excavation was continued in 1967.

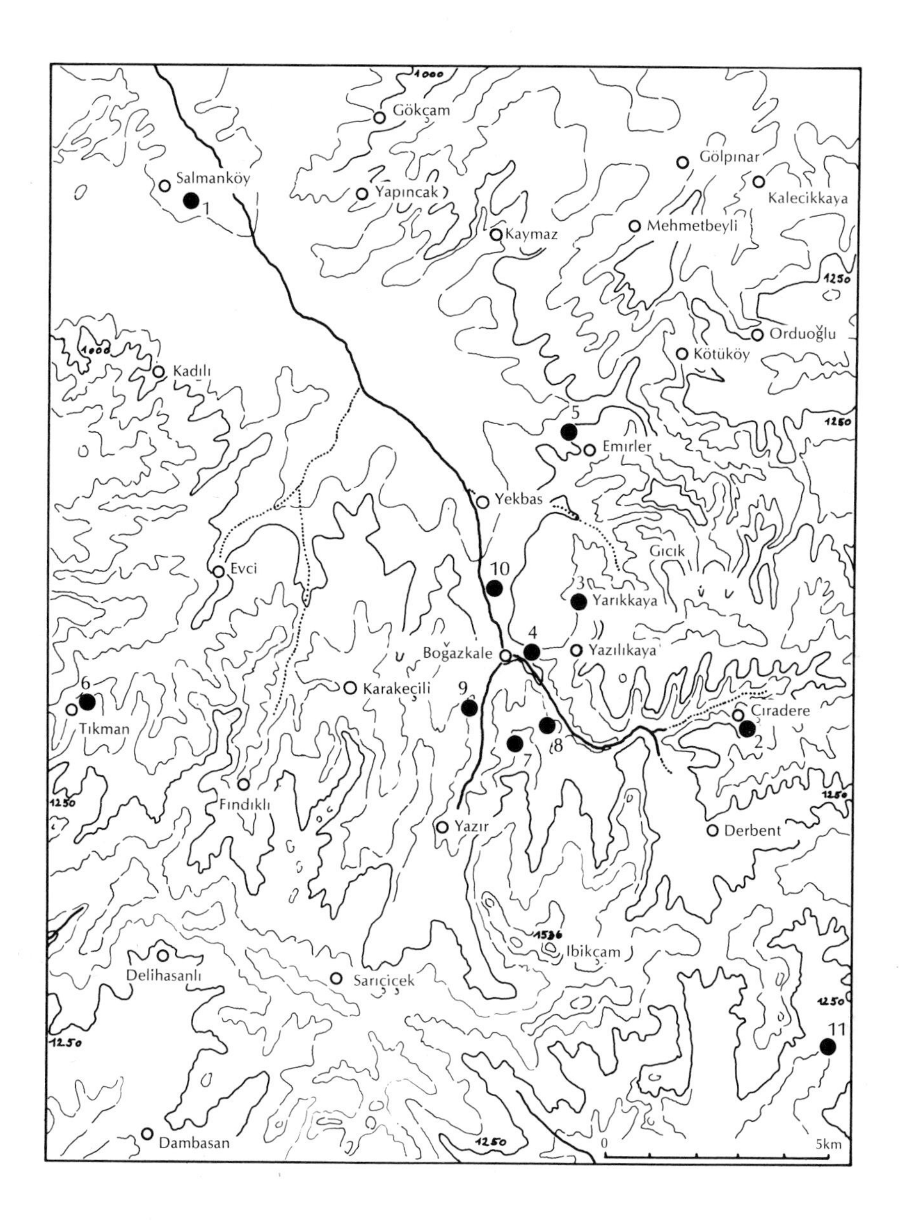

Figure 4. Map of Chalcolithic and Early Bronze Age sites in the vicinity of Boğazköy (Boğazkale): 1. Salmanköy; 2. Çiradere; 3. Yarıkkaya; 4. Büyükkaya; 5. Emirler; 6. Tıkman; 7. Outside Yerkapı; 8. Above Kayali Boğazı; 9. Kormukaya; 10. Near the Boğazköy-su; 11. Kamışçıkte-Hüyük

These hamlets and farmsteads of the Early Bronze Age in the neighborhood of Boğazköy are settlements not directly connected with Hattusha and cannot, therefore, be included in its early history. They merely prove settlement in the area of which the city was later to become a part. But we enter a new phase with the transitional period which led from the third into the second millennium B.C. Two places within the city area were now settled: one on the rock of Büyükkale, represented by levels IVd and Va-f, the other at the foot of the northern spur of this hill, on a terrace in the immediate vicinity of a perennial spring (fig. 5). In the latter case, the water and the proximity to cultivable land were presumable inducements to settlement; at Büyükkale it must have been the natural defense offered by the rocky hill. We do not know whether the two sites were connected from the start, in spite of their separate locations, or whether they existed as independent communities, to be united at a later stage. They were, at any rate, the nucleus of the city—as far as we can judge today—and mark the beginning of its history. The very choice of their location points to two advantages which during the entire history of Hattusha proved to be important factors: the occurrence of water in an otherwise arid region and a terrain favorable to the exploitation of natural defenses.

In both these locations later construction disrupted the earlier levels to such an extent that we have only isolated wall sections of most of the houses, but no complete ground plans. For the same reason it is impossible to determine the size and the layout of these settlements. Nevertheless, it would certainly be wrong to dismiss them as insignificant or even primitive communities. A house of Büyükkale level Vc is well enough preserved to give some idea about its size and interior subdivision (fig. 6). It had at least eight rooms on different levels, adjusted to the slightly sloping ground and terraced accordingly. Staircases built of stone and covered with plaster connected the upper and the lower rooms. A room containing an oven and a hearth is clearly a kitchen, and the adjoining room, with its large clay vessels, must have been a storage room. In two places charred wooden doors were found

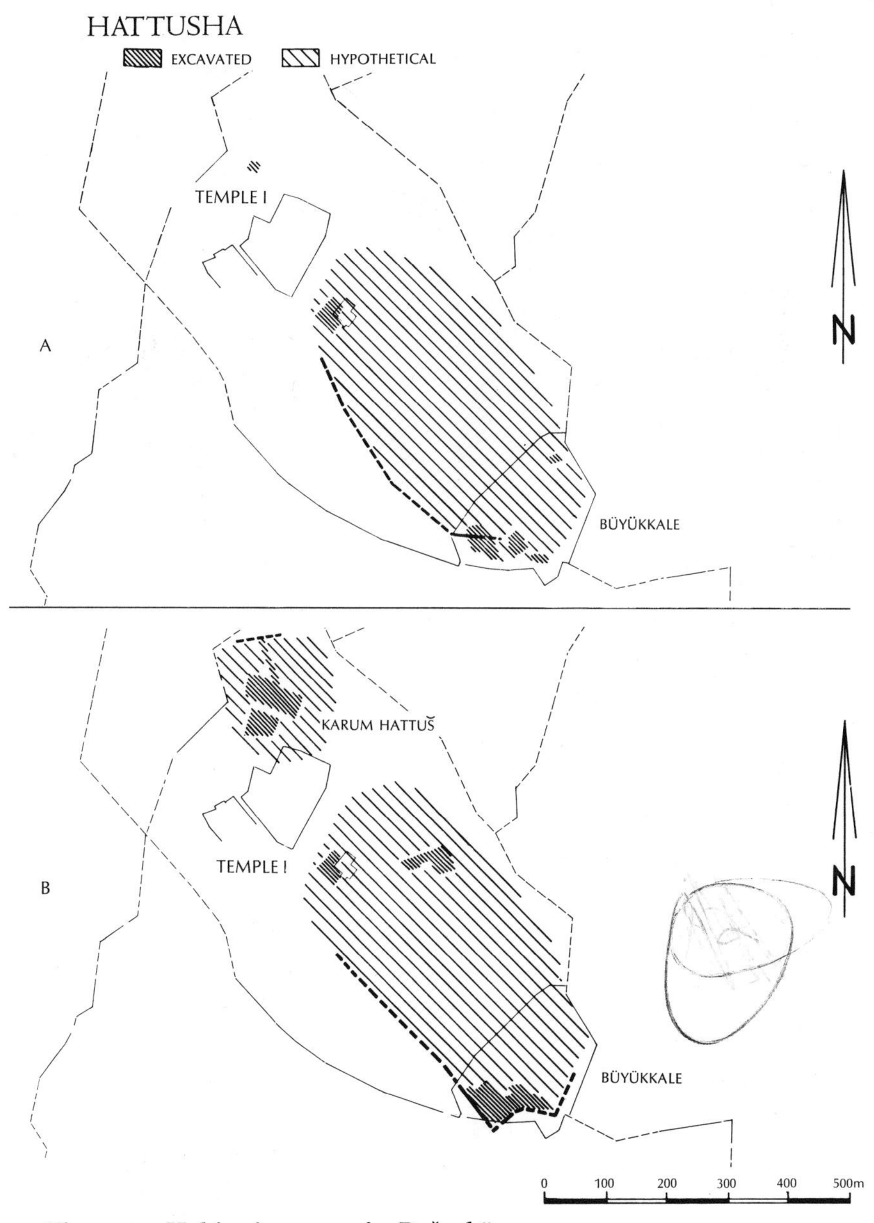

Figure 5. Habitation areas in Boğazköy:
A. in the early Bronze III period. B. in the Old Assyrian period

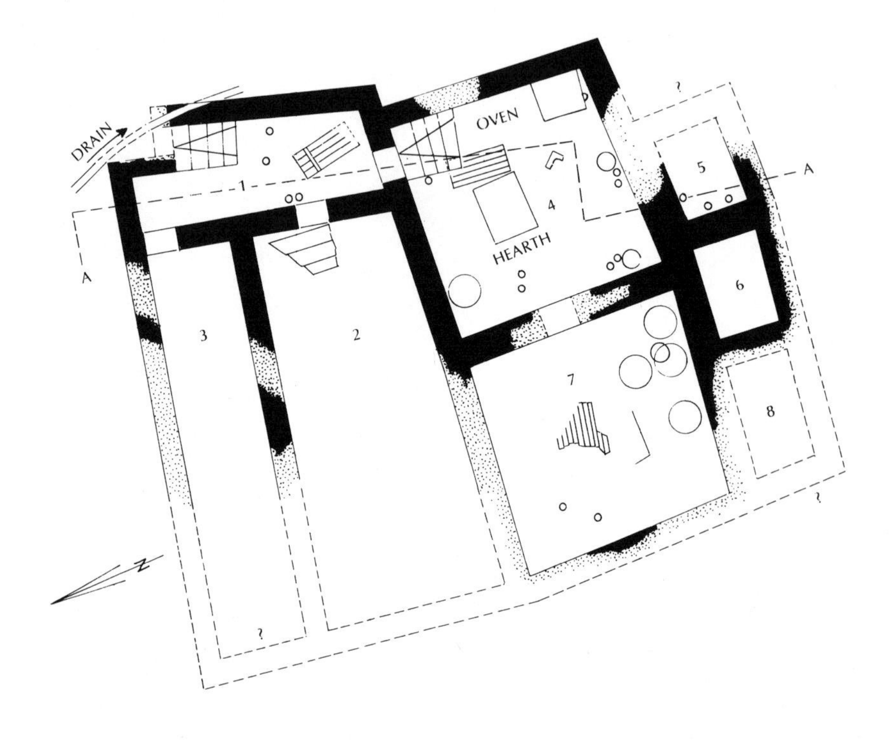

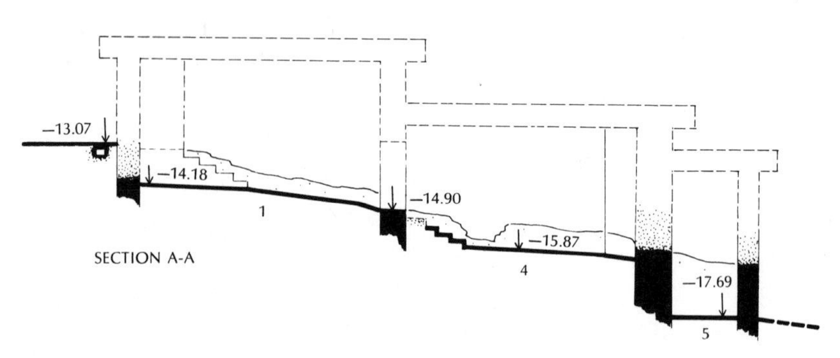

Figure 6. House plan of Büyükkale level Vc

as they had fallen to the ground when knocked from their pivots during the destruction of the house. The better preserved one measures 1.80 by 0.85 meters, a quite respectable size. The imposing building, which measured about 19 by 15 meters, contained a wealth of finds, especially in pottery. A giant-spouted pitcher has handles of unparalleled design, decorated with rams' heads and lion protomes. On the shoulder on each side of the base of the handle is an ibex in high relief (plate 5).

Yet it is not the finds, instructive as they are, which lend special significance to this house, but rather its ground plan, the interior subdivision, and the adaptation to the sloping ground. The free-standing building, the juxtaposition of the rooms upon the principle of simple addition, the habit of staggering the partition walls instead of continuing them in a straight line, the use of offsets in the outer wall—here to be seen at least in the front of the house—and, finally, the terracing of the ground: all these are full-fledged, Old Anatolian architectural traits which remained dominant in central Asia Minor for nearly a millennium until the end of Hittite Hattusha. These architectural principles we shall meet again, although on a monumental scale, in the buildings of the 14th and 13th centuries B.C., which in this respect betray themselves as descendants of pre-Hittite architecture, of the local, native ways of building. To my knowledge, this building of Büyükkale level Vc is the oldest extant witness to this long-lasting tradition. The size and the number of rooms in this instance prove, however, that we are not yet at the beginning of the series. This house surely takes its place in an evolution which starts in earlier, still-unexplored stages.

Level V of Büyükkale has six sublevels, Vf-Va (Va being the latest) in the area investigated. The house just discussed belongs, as noted above, to Vc, a settlement which perished in a great conflagration, as attested by a heavy, burned layer in the entire excavated area. The settlements of levels Vf-Vc on Büyükkale and 9-8d on the northern terrace of the city are essentially contemporary with levels IV and III of the kārum Kanesh of Kültepe. This is proved by ample ceramic finds and particularly by the

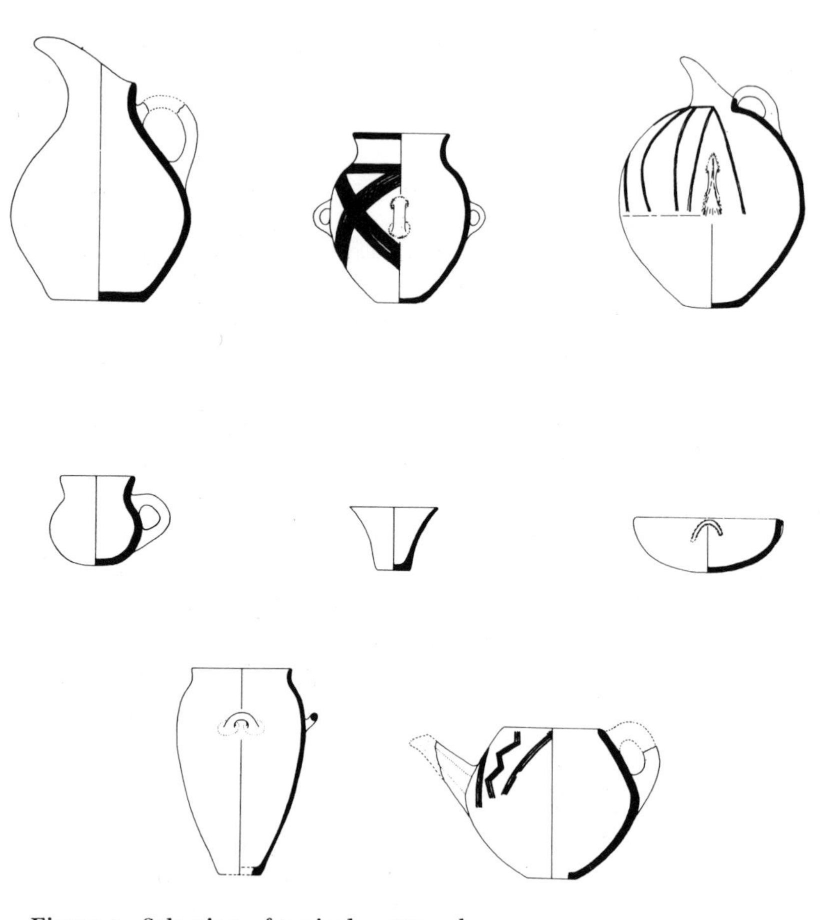

Figure 7. Selection of typical pottery shapes:
A. lower city, House on the Slope area level 9

co-existence of hand and wheel-made pottery, although here—in the north—details of shape and workmanship differ somewhat from the types current in the southern culture represented by Kanesh (fig. 7). The beginnings of Büyükkale V and the lower city 9, however, may go back a little further than kārum Kanesh IV, presumably to the final phase of the third millennium B.C. This, then, represents the earliest hitherto known occupation

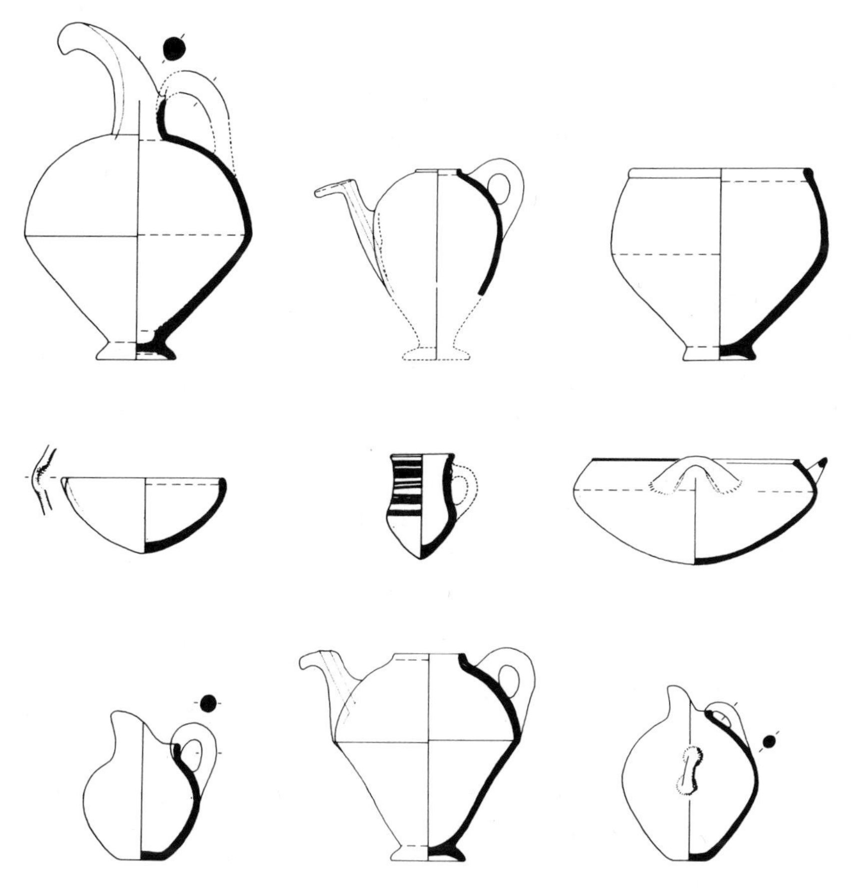

B. lower city, House on the Slope area levels 8b-a

within the city area of Hattusha, too late to be identified with the Hatti of King Pamba which appears in the above-mentioned text of Naram-Sin. We thus at present have no archaeological evidence which might convert the legendary tradition into historical reality.

In the following, second period of the history of the city, the focal points of the occupation are in the two areas already mentioned: Büyükkale with levels Vb-a and IVd and the terrace at the foot of the northwest slope with levels 8b and 8a. In the later phase of this period, however, the area of occupation is widened considerably. The site gradually acquires the character of a city, not only in size, but also in its internal administration and organization. These facts, to be studied in some detail later on, allow us to see this development as a particularly important period in the history of the city. There is, of course, no sudden break with the past, but rather an unmistakable evolution of the local culture based on the achievements of the first period. In level 8b of the north slope, the pottery, e.g., is still very similar to that of level 9. Hand-made ware still occurs, but is gradually outnumbered by wheel-made ware. In the later phase of this period—level 8a of the northwest slope and level IVd on Büyükkale—wheel-made ware predominates and is superior in form and quality. The potter's art in fact reaches a peak during this period. Nevertheless, the syntax of these vases is thoroughly based on tradition. New qualities are the tightening of the shapes, the relative proportions of the elements of the vases, the noticeable dependency of clay vessels on metallic prototypes and the virtuosity of the potter in using his new device, the wheel.

In architecture, tradition also prevails. This is quite apparent, for example, in a house of level IVd on Büyükkale which has a a nucleus of at least six rooms and a court (fig. 8). To its south side, in a second stage of building, small and very small irregular rooms were added. They were used for commercial purposes since they contained many storage vessels and a large number of stamped, clay bullae which had once been attached to wooden crates and boxes (fig. 9). The nucleus of this house, in subdivision and layout, is very similar to that of the house of the first period discussed earlier.

The settlement on Büyükkale (IVd) was protected by a fortification wall, parts of which were exposed in 1964. It consisted of a solid, rough-stone foundation with a superstructure of mudbrick. It is still uncertain whether this wall extended far enough down the slope to include the settlement at the northern base of the rock. Stray finds, however, suggest that the slope, especially its milder

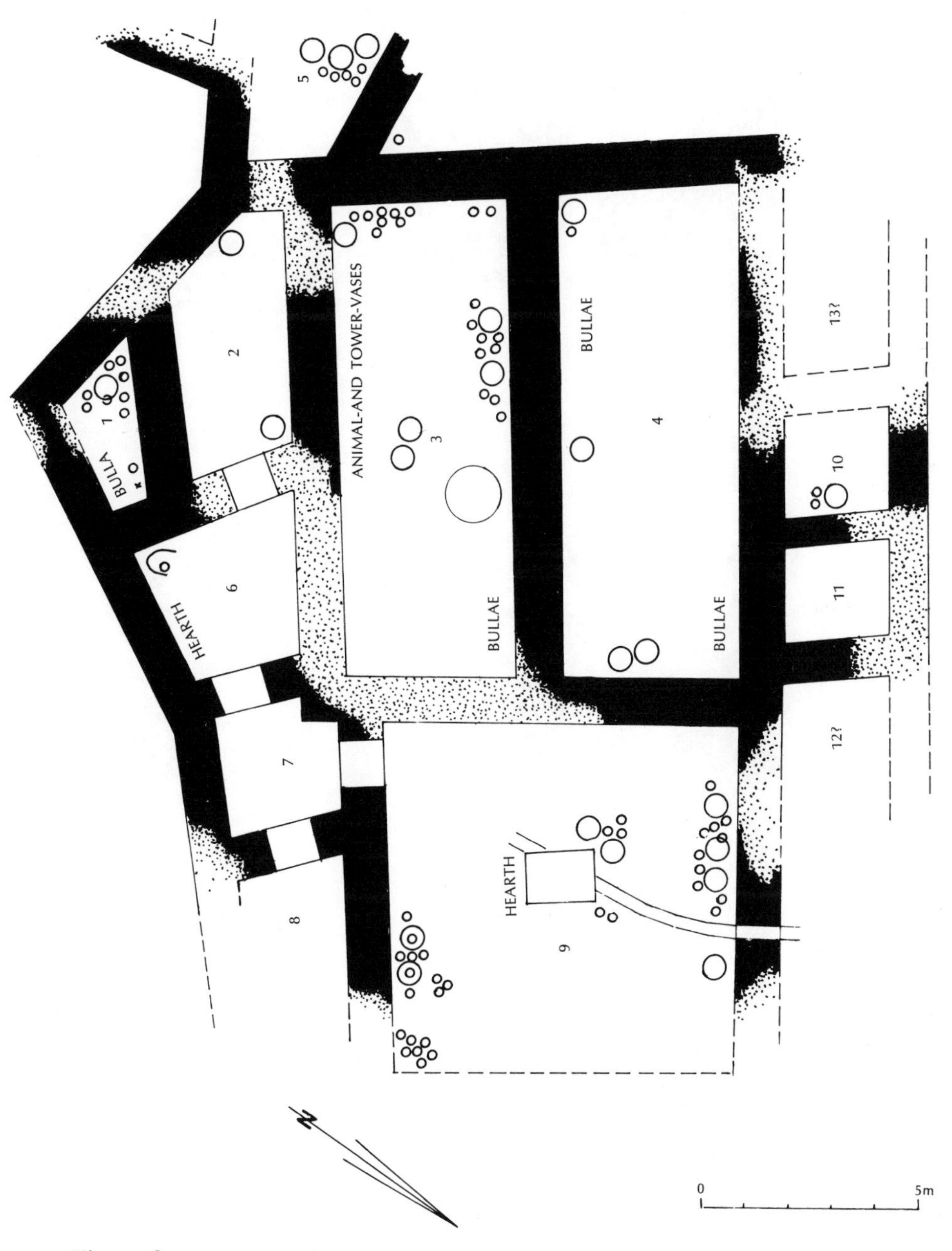

Figure 8.
House plan of Büyükkale level IVd

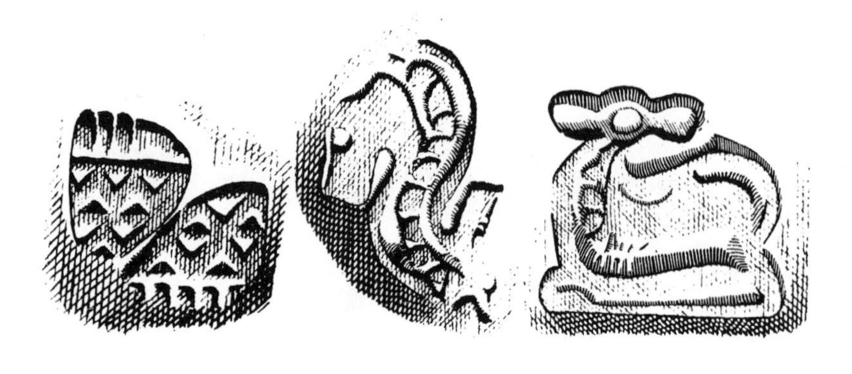

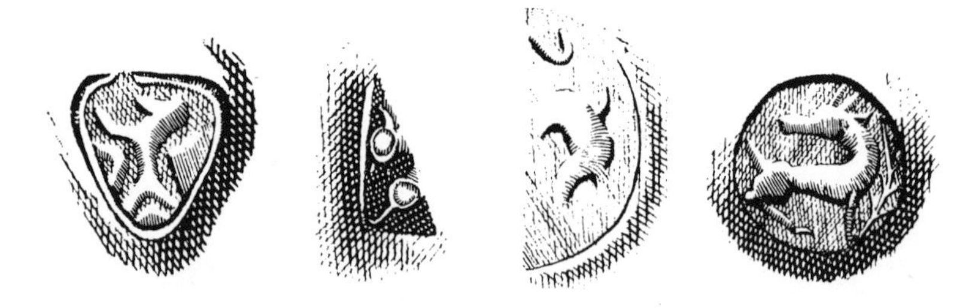

Figure 9. A-C. Bullae with stamp seal impressions, Büyükkale level IVd. Diameter 0.009-0.018 m.

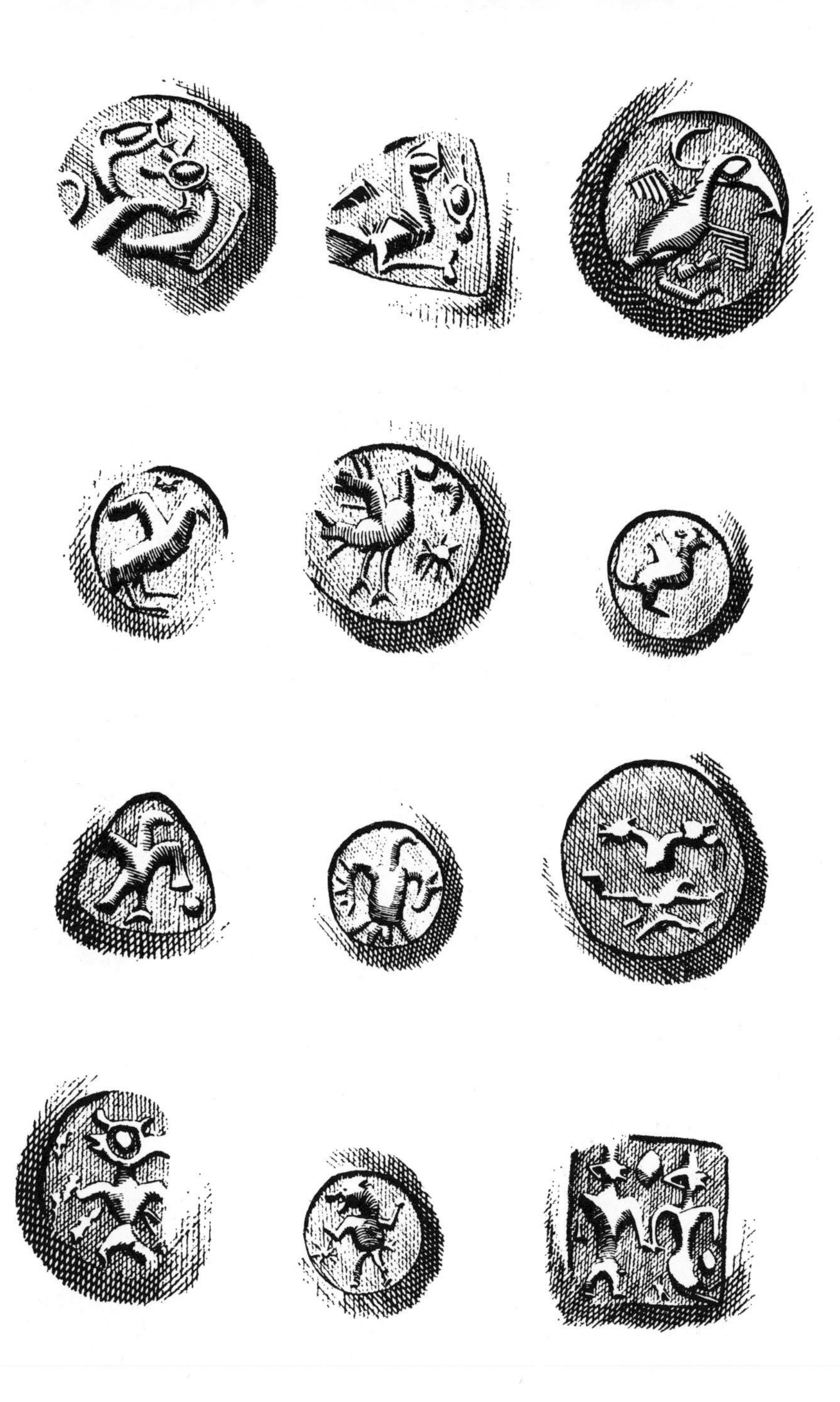

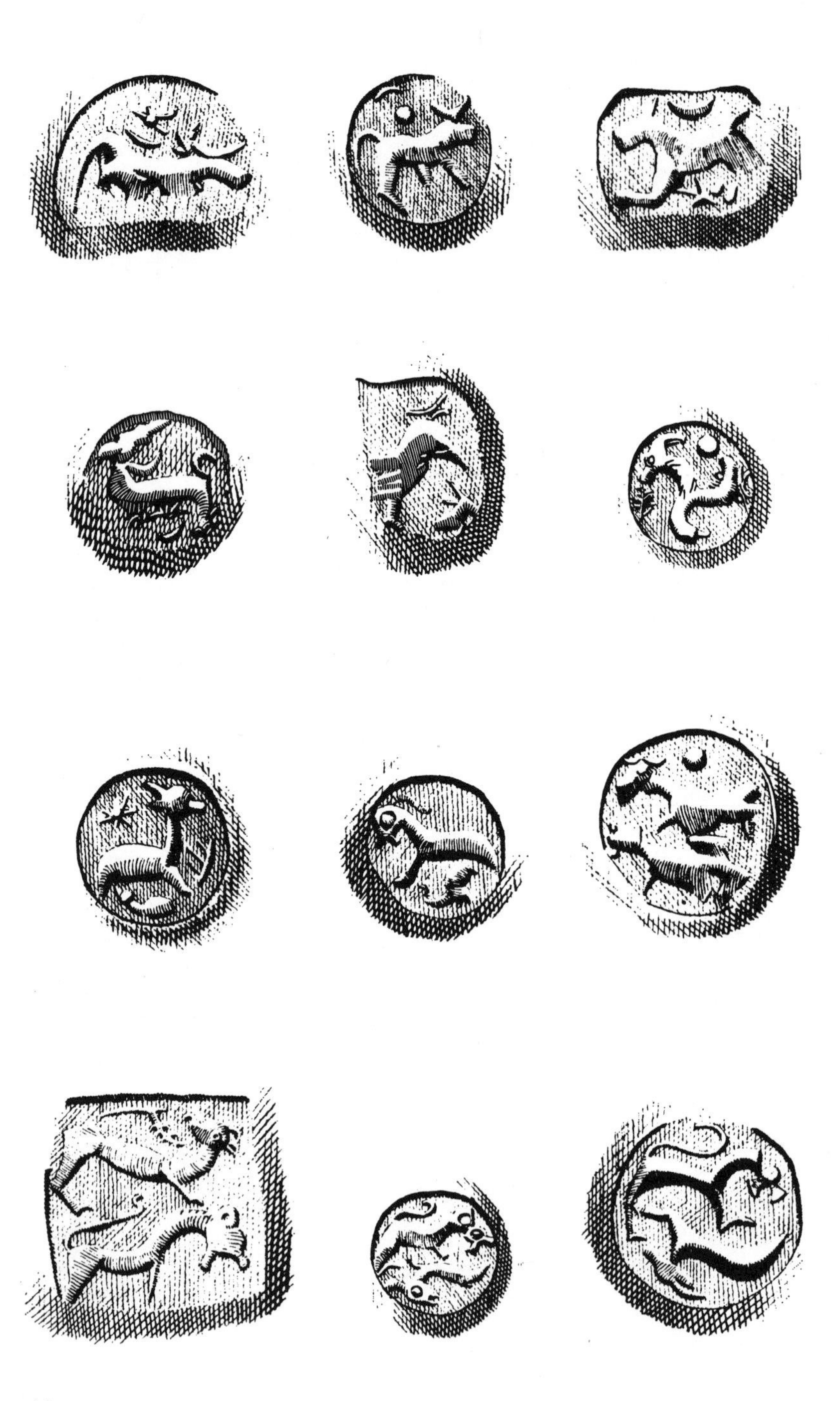

inclines and possibly also some artificially leveled terraces, could have been entirely covered with buildings. It would seem possible that in this period, the previously isolated settlement areas (of period 1) coalesced to form a single large community.

During the later phase of this period of the city's history, a settlement was founded on hitherto nearly unoccupied ground farther north, on two terraces nearest the valley. Its size can be approximately assessed, although only a part of it has until now been excavated as a unit. The results, however, are instructive enough. The habitation area is crowded, but has some degree of regularity. All the buildings are uniformly oriented northeast-southwest and consist of complexes of varying though respectable size with a considerable number of rooms (fig. 10). Each unit is bordered on all four sides by paved alleys, usually provided with drainage channels. From these alleys, one entered directly into the courtyard through a special passage. Around the court were the individual rooms whose respective purposes are indicated by the presence of hearths, ovens, and vessels for storage and supplies (plate 6a). The occupant of each house was obviously at liberty to arrange his establishment freely within the given limits; however, the general layout was planned at a higher level and on a communal basis. Nobody was allowed to add to his estate at will, but he was bound to the regulations of a collective community. The great number of rooms in the houses is not only due to economic needs, including the establishment of offices, but also the result of architectural restriction to a single storey of building. The relatively weak stone socles which supported equally thin walls of mud-brick show quite clearly that the houses could not have been more than one storey high. Almost all of these houses, it may be noted, have three phases of building, noticeable in that the floors and the hearths were raised twice without important structural alterations in the buildings themselves. Judging from the life span and strength of modern Anatolian houses, which in material and structure are largely similar to these old buildings, the latter can hardly have lasted more than half a century.

The ground plans of the houses are never unfamiliar. They

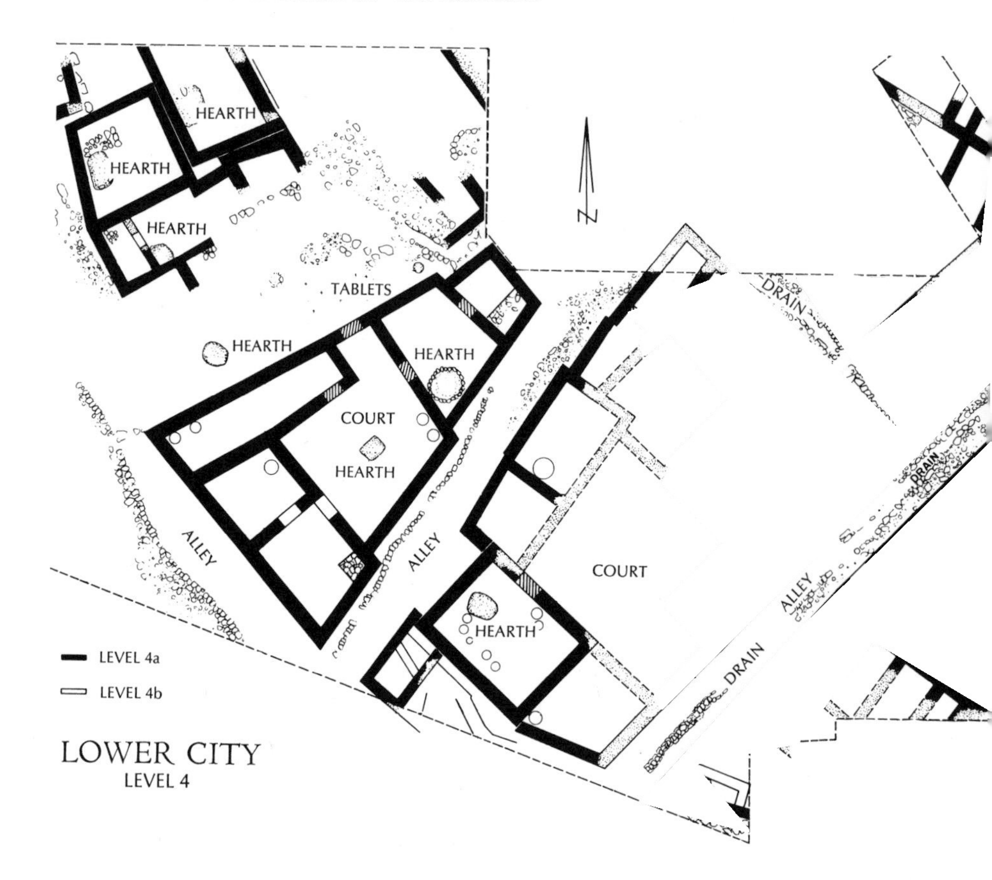

Figure 10. Plan of the kārum Hattush, lower city level 4

varied somewhat in details, but basically they followed the form and structure of those we met in the earliest settlement on the site of Hattusha. There is little doubt that these houses and, indeed, those of the entire settlement so far as it has been excavated, were erected by local workmen following old, native methods of house building. And yet, they were building for foreign residents, some of whom we even know by name. There are, for instance, one Da-ā, son of Il-Bāni, and one Shamashtaklaku, of whom we have cuneiform texts in Old Assyrian from this settle-

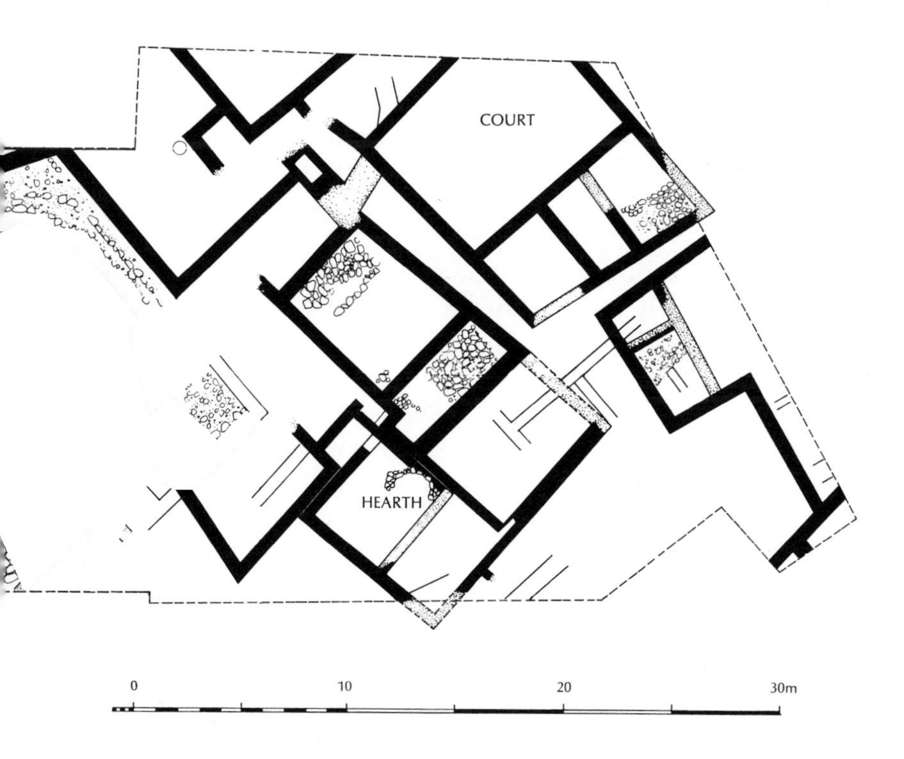

ment. In two instances, the tablets were so numerous that we may see them as small archives of the respective residents who were the heads of trading firms. Of the Old Assyrian documents found in Boğazköy (plate 6b), only one comes from Büyükkale, two are from other parts of the city, but about sixty from the settlement just described. Here, no doubt, the Assyrian trading organization had its center, here was the kārum Hattush, the trading post of Hattush. These documents contain only Assyrian names, no native ones. The impressions of cylinder seals on the envelopes show, without exception, Mesopotamian, non-Anatolian motifs. Among the very few extant original seals of this type, there is, nevertheless, an occasional specimen of an indigenous style, while the numerous stamp seals are entirely of local provenance (plate 7). In this period, then, the site steps out of the prehistoric darkness into the light of history. Its name occurs for the first time and in its Hattian form. Commercial and legal transactions contained in the documents show that Hattush was incorporated into the organization of the Old Assyrian trading colonies in Anatolia. To judge by the available texts, in this case, the faraway "City," meaning Assur itself on the Tigris, played a more important role than the relatively nearby kārum Kanesh, the main Assyrian colony in Anatolia. This does not mean, however, that there were no relations with kārum Kanesh. Hattush occurs quite often among the thousands of business documents found at Kültepe. So there was trade.

What period are we dealing with and how does this city of Hattush compare with its contemporary counterparts in Central Anatolia? Every attempt at a classification will have to start from the important and fruitful results of the excavations carried out by our Turkish colleagues in the kārum Kanesh, the main Assyrian settlement. It is well known that this principal colony has two distinct phases of development: kārum Kanesh level II which with its innumerable trade records represents the *floruit* of the colony, and the more recent kārum level Ib with far fewer records, showing a considerable fall off in trade and activity, and presumably also a change in the relationship between the Assyrians and the indigenous dynasties. The settlement of level II was destroyed by a great fire; the reconstruction in level Ib took place after a brief interval which cannot yet be measured in exact numbers of years. These are stratigraphic facts which have been secured by numerous observations at Kültepe. They cannot simply be pushed aside, as has recently been done by Paul Garelli in his book *Les Assyriens en Cappadoce,* in favor of theories which are incompatible with the archaeological data.

In the opinion of Garelli, there is only a single kārum Kanesh, namely, that of level II, and no second phase of this colony. To him, the business documents found in level Ib are contemporary with those of level II, stirred up from the earlier level in the course of later building operations. The later building level actually would have belonged to a period after the fall of the kārum Kanesh. The observations at Hattush are entirely at variance with this theory and speak undoubtedly for the correctness of the interpretation of the excavators of Kültepe. This deserves a brief justification in the present context.

The Assyrian trading establishment of Hattush, judging by the archaeological context of the tablets, turned out to be contemporary with kārum Kanesh Ib. The pottery at the two sites is related and many of the shapes are identical. This holds good not only for individual pieces, but also for groups of vessels customarily used together as "tableware." There are also parallels in ritual objects. A lead figure of a male deity from Hattush (plate 8a) has a counterpart in kārum Kanesh Ib, and casting moulds of a goddess standing on an animal and holding animals in her hands, a *Potnia Therôn,* occur in Hattush as well as in Kanesh (plate 8b). Moreover, the two sites practice similar ways of building. Decisive is what Heinrich Otten and Kemal Balkan proved. The occurrence of certain names of merchants and of specific Assyrian *limus,* that is, annual officials, in the Old Assyrian documents from Hattush makes them contemporary with those from Alişar and kārum Kanesh Ib, thus dating them to the time of Shamshi-Adad I of Assyria or—in terms of the so-called short chronology—to the years between 1749 and 1717 B.C.. This then is a certified period for the existence of the trading colony at Hattush. It must, however, have been quite a bit older and may have reached back before the middle of the 18th century, probably even well into the 19th century B.C. In the tablets of kārum Kanesh II, the older and main phase of the Central Assyrian trading colony, Hattush occurs a number of times, e.g. as the residence of business partners. Hattush, then, was already involved in the business transactions and the site of a trading colony. Yet, unlike Kanesh, Hattush has not yielded a single trade document from this older period of the kind contemporary with kārum Kanesh II. The same is true of the site of Alişar midway between Hattush and Kanesh. Seventy tablets and fragments are known from that site, all of which—so far as they are datable—again belong to the period of kārum Kanesh Ib. These facts are apt to raise some questions though by no means of such radical implications as Garelli's. It is astonishing indeed that for the *floruit* of the Assyrian trading organization we have documents from one place only, namely, from Kanesh itself. Their number runs into thousands and is constantly increased in the course of the continuing excavations. The documents, on the other hand, from places outside the kārum Kanesh, namely, Alişar and Hattush, belong precisely to that phase which is marked by recession and a considerable shrinkage of business transactions. We should have expected the chronological and regional distribution of such tablets to have been just the reverse. I am, however, convinced that in this case, statistics are deceptive, at least in Hattush.

The finds of levels Vb, Va, and the older IVd on Büyükkale, and of 8b on the northwest slope of the citadel evidently are roughly contemporary with kārum Kanesh II. A number of lion-shaped vessels from Hattush (plate 9) and vases of very typical forms (plate 10a) found together with them either have exact parallels at Kanesh or, especially in the case of the animal-shaped vessels, are so close to counterparts at Kanesh that they cannot be very far apart in time. This Hattush of the kārum Kanesh II period, however, passes into the later phase of period 2 of the history of the city without a break; the habitation area is merely expanded. The catastrophe which hit Kanesh II left Hattush untouched. Hattush has no corresponding conflagration level (destruction level). It has no business documents of the relevant trading companies, and this was no doubt due to the fact that no incident had befallen the settlement to bury the tablets under a layer of conflagration debris as had happened at the kārum Kanesh. The records, instead, remained in the hands of their owners who kept them as long as needed, and at the end of the transaction and after expiration of its terms either destroyed them, or moved them somewhere else. We cannot expect large holdings of such records to have survived. In Hattush, too, only those records survived which happened to be in the establishments just before the Assyrian trading colony perished in a violent destruction. This event occurred at the end of level IVd of Büyükkale, of 8a on the northwest slope, and at the end of 4, the latest phase on the lower city terrace. According to the date given by the tablets—a date *post quem*—kārum Hattush was destroyed in the late 18th century B.C.

This must have meant not merely the fall of an Assyrian trading colony, but of a whole city whose actual core consisted of a settlement of Hattian residents living under the rule of a native Hattian dynasty. Such a pattern is also known for a number of other cities of Central Anatolia of this period. In each case, the Assyrian colony was an adjunct of a native community. We cannot yet prove this in detail for Hattush, but very probably we may consider Büyükkale as the seat of the prince and the settlement at the foot of this citadel as that of his Anatolian subjects. The Assyrian trade-post was a close adjunct and neighbor. This entire community fell victim to a great catastrophe attested everywhere by a heavy burned layer which covers the ruined houses. Not a single building was re-erected after this destruction.

We may confidently identify this fall of the city of Hattush with an event in the literary tradition, *viz.* the conquest of the city of King Pijushti of Hatti by King Anitta of Kushshar-Nesha which we know from a text quoted verbatim in the preceding chapter: "and during the night I took it by assault. But in its place I sowed weeds." Anitta belongs in the exact period referred to by the Old Assyrian records of Hattush. A document from Alişar makes Anitta contemporary with the latest phase of the Old Assyrian trading colonies. Originally a local prince, he rose to become the ruler over a kingdom which included a number of previously independent principalities. Finds of the last twenty years allow us to trace his career in some, though not great, detail. One stage on the road of the conqueror Anitta was the capture and the destruction of Hattush.

Somewhat over a hundred years later, the Hittite Great King Hattushili I chose these ruins as the site upon which to build the capital of his empire and to establish his residence. We know his motives for deciding on a location relatively so far to the north in Anatolia. And it is clear that the area of the old city of Hattush commended itself because of its natural advantages. Perhaps some of its old traditions may also have played a part.

The natural advantages are particularly striking when one views the city area from the northern valley. It is a strongly diversified terrain with a rise of nearly 300 yards in just over a mile. This area, with an over-all slope from south to north, is broken up by numerous valleys, depressions, rocks, inclines, and plateaus which made building operations rather difficult. But against this drawback stand major advantages. The domain of the city is set off from its surroundings by deep gorges carrying water throughout the year. It was a natural stronghold which, with artificial fortifications, would provide effective protection, and it had an ample supply of water.

Of the Old Hittite Hattusha of the 16th and 15th centuries, the third period of the city's history, regrettably little has been recovered by the excavations as yet. On Büyükkale, level IVc (with three sublevels) belongs to this period; in the northern part of the city—roughly where the kārum Hattush had once been—level 3 (with two sublevels) is the pertinent stratum. Surely the kings held court on Büyükkale, yet of the residence only insignificant remnants survive since much was demolished in the course of later building operations. The fragmentary buildings discovered there and in the northern part of the city make it evident that the architecture still adhered to the forms familiar from the older (first and second) periods.

Limited though our information about the details of Old Hittite Hattusha may be, at least the size of the city site at the end of this period—that is, during the 15th century—is sufficiently clear. It included the area defined at the south by the towering fortress of Büyükkale and in the north by the junction of two valleys, the eastern Büyükkaya-deresi and the western Kızlarkaya-deresi. This whole region, of a maximum length of 3/4 mile and a maximum width of slightly over 1/4 mile, was enclosed by a city wall which we may perhaps consider the work of Great King Hantili who ruled about 1520 B.C. He is known to have fortified

Hattusha, but in any case, whoever erected the fortifications followed older principles of military architecture. The city wall, 8 meters thick, stands on an artificial rampart and consists of a high substructure of coarse masonry built with an inner and outer face connected by cross-walls. The resulting compartments were filled with rubble, adding up to a solid substructure which carried the superstructure of mudbrick, the latter rising to a height of at least 6 meters. This type of "casemate-wall" is known from a much earlier period; such a construction at Alişar dates to the 18th century B.C. The same is true of the posterns in the city wall of Old Hittite Hattusha, subterranean passages built in corbeled technique. At least one example of this type of postern occurs in Alişar, again as early as the 18th century. So, the Old Hittite kings followed native usage also in building their fortifications, although on the stony and rocky ground of Hattusha, masonry predominated over constructions of mudbrick.

To erect the city wall on an artificial rampart higher than the ground in front, thus forming an effective glacis, was demanded by the art of warfare of that time. At the siege of Urshu which took place in the latter years of the reign of Hattushili I, a battering ram and a siege tower are already mentioned.

The temples of the Old Hittite city, partly known to us from literary traditions, have not yet been located. From the document of Hattushili I referred to in Chapter I, to quote but one of the Old Hittite texts, we know that several sanctuaries must have existed. The text mentions a temple of the Sun Goddess of Arinna and one of Mezulla. A temple of the Weather God also occurs in other texts; it may have stood on the same site as the largest temple of the city of the 14th and 13th centuries B.C. Should this assumption prove to be correct, then it would remain forever beyond our reach since the later sanctuary stands on an impenetrable terrace constructed of enormous boulders.

Within level IVc of Büyükkale, there is an extensive burned destruction level. Since it belongs to the phase of Büyükkale IVc3, it is considerably too early for the destruction of Hattusha which written sources report for the time of Great King Tuthaliya III.

At present, we have no material evidence directly connected with this event. But there are indirect repercussions in the archaeological sequence, for immediately after 1400 B.C., as will be explained in detail in Chapter III, a thorough remodeling started on the entire lower plateau of Büyükkale—the royal palace—and at the same time, the city itself was rebuilt. This is level IVb of Büyükkale and level 2 of the lower city. These proceedings usher in that period of the history of the city which we shall call the fourth, the period of the 14th and 13th centuries during which Hattusha was the capital of the Hittite Great Empire.

During this time span of barely 200 years, Hattusha acquired the character of a great city of its age, the impressive seat of an empire and a court which belonged among the leading powers of the world at that time. It survives in a series of monuments, some never buried, others recovered by excavations. The dominant features are five great temples, an ambitious expansion of the old city site, and the royal court, the saray of the Great Kings of Büyükkale to be discussed in the following chapter. We will here briefly examine some aspects and details.

The extension incorporated into the city an area double the size of the site of the old town. In laying out the wall, the builders skillfully exploited the ridge above the steep slopes of the Büyükkaya-deresi in the east and the Yazır-deresi in the west. In the south, a natural depression at the highest point, today called Yerkapı (fig. 11; plate 11) was artificially deepened and widened to form a fosse which isolated the town from the adjoining plateau further to the south. At Kızlarkaya, on the one hand, and at Büyükkale on the other, the new city-wall was tied in with the old city. At least five gates, three on the west side and two on the east, gave access from the outside to this new part of the city. They all represent the same type: towers flanking the outer gateway, gates with parabolic arches formed by large blocks, a gate-chamber which could be closed on both sides by heavy, wooden, bronze-covered folding doors (fig. 12; plate 12). Both sets of doors opened to the inside of the gate-chamber allowing defense in either direction. Inside the gate-chamber, the holes into which the bolts fitted and

Figure 11. City wall near Yerkapı. Reconstruction

the door sockets are still visible, and to the left and right, beam-holes show where the heavy cross-bars were fixed in place to secure the closed doors. These are, therefore, relatively simple gates, in fact just openings at right angles to the city wall without any special strategic refinements to block entry. But this weakness is offset by the two strong flanking towers. In addition, the enemy approaching the gates from the outside had no choice but to follow a ramp along the city wall to reach the gate entrance. The attacker was thus exposed to the defenders posted on the *chemin de ronde* of the city wall.

Archive K of the royal citadel has yielded a document which relates (exceptionally, in Hittite literature) an incident of real life, here concerning a city gate. It is an instruction to the Hazannu, the "Burgomaster" of the capital Hattusha. Its author is King Arnuwanda. It is not clear whether he is the third king of this name, which would date the text to the latter decades of the 13th century, or an earlier king of the same name, which would mean the second half of the 15th or the 14th century. It reads:

> "You, Burgomaster, be very careful in matters of the guard, and in Hattusha the guard shall be well controlled."

And further on:

> "When they lift the copper bolts on the gate in the morning . . . when you have sent your son or servant to open the

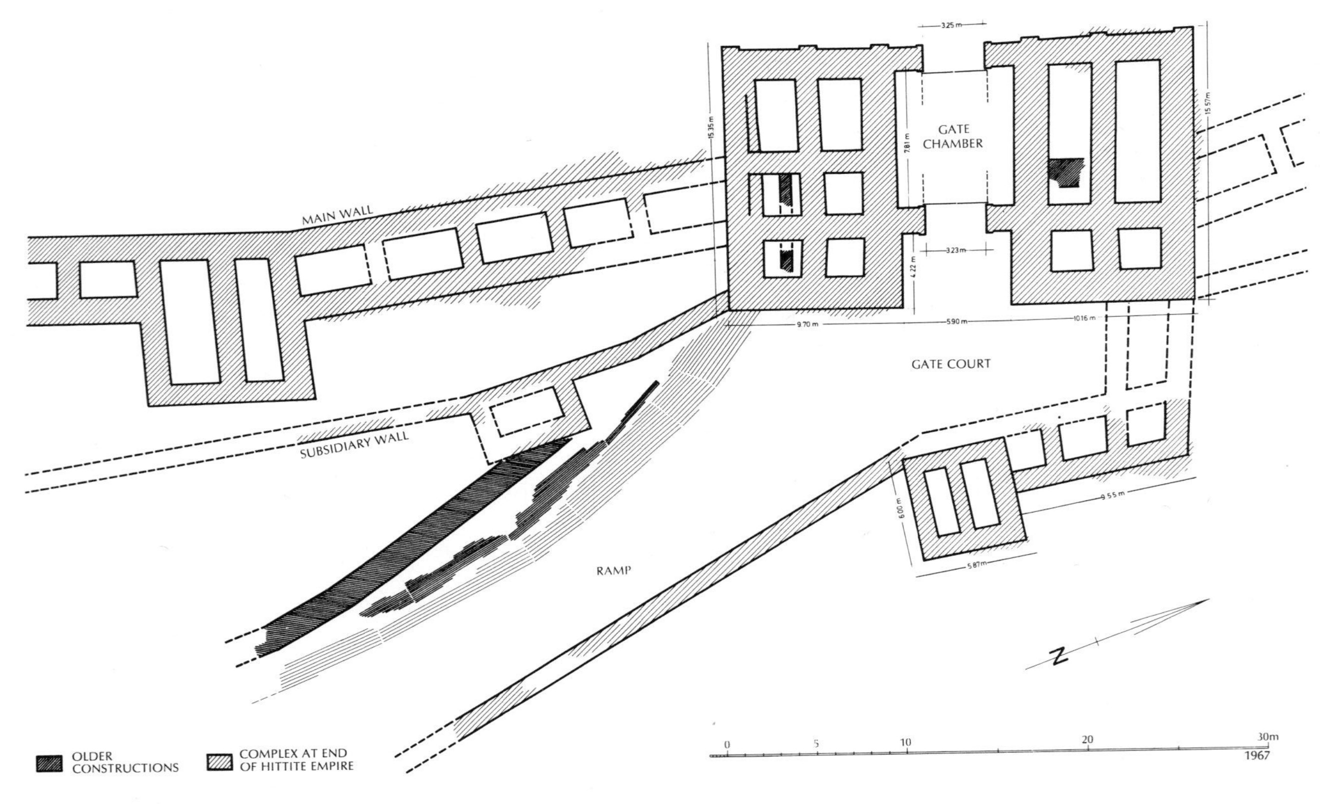

Figure 12. Plan of the Royal Gate

> doors, when the seal on the gate 'turns,' then afterwards a man from Hatti or a commanding officer, or whoever is on duty, shall together examine the seal at the gate and open the gate accordingly. They shall carry the copper bolts back to the house and put them down in their place."

Some passages of this text are not easy to understand, but it is clear that gates were not only carefully closed at night, but also that the locks were always sealed, and that the closing of the doors in the evening and the opening in the morning was performed under the strict supervision of functionaries for whom the Hazannu, the Burgomaster, was responsible to the King. Considering that the old and new town between them had at least seven gates, these people were sufficiently occupied in discharging this duty. Finally, a letter found in 1964 in Hattusha testifies to the care with which the fortifications were tended and maintained. It was addressed to the king by an official called Kashshu to report on the inspection of fortifications in need of repair.

The fortification wall of the new city closely follows the model of that of the old city. It, too, is a casemate wall erected on a high rampart. However, unlike the fortifications of the old city, it has a lower wall built in front of the main wall, with towers corresponding to intervals between the main towers. The course of the walls was not determined by practical considerations only. This is most noticeable where the wall reaches the highest point of the city, at the so-called Yerkapı. Here we have an interrelated, strategic design: the main wall and the lower wall standing on a high artificial rampart, a postern leading straight through the rampart for a length of 71 meters, and two staircases leading down along the paved outer slope of the rampart to the right and left. The postern and the gate-tower located exactly above it form the axis. The stairs make identical angles to this axis; their extension upwards meets the main wall at points where its course changes at an equal angle on both sides. This is a strictly symmetrical and consistent design, with each element firmly fixed in the total complex—a kind of planning directed by much more than considerations of efficiency (fig. 11, plate 11).

We may perhaps reconstruct this city wall on the analogy of two small finds which came to light in 1957. They are fragments of two vessels, one of them very large and more than half preserved, the other preserved only in a rim fragment of a white slipped and polished vessel. This rim is shaped like a crenellated wall surmounted by projecting, rectangular towers, also crenellated (plate 10b). These towers, two storeys high, have four oblong openings—two at the front and one on each side. The longitudinal beams which appear in the face of the wall are indicated by engraved lines, while the double ends of the crossbeams project outwards. It seems most likely that this is a miniature imitation of contemporary fortification architecture. The vases were found in a context which dates them to the 14th century.

Within the so-called new town, there are four monumental buildings which we may consider as temples. Since in the same period of the city's history a large sanctuary was also erected in the center of the old city, we should here briefly discuss religious buildings in the Hittite capital in general, at the risk of repeating some well-known facts.

Of the four temples of the new city, three are located not far apart in the eastern zone of the highest part of the town (plate 13a). An enclosure wall, traced for some length, suggests that they all stood together in a *temenos*. In their choice of the location for each temple, the builders exhibited great skill. An observer standing on the wall at Yerkapı and looking down on them immediately feels that they lie exactly where they should, that their sites have been chosen with an extraordinary sensitivity to the terrain and the setting. Each temple is moved forward to the edge of a small projecting plateau. Thus, each one of these buildings is set off against its surroundings and is visible from a long way away. The view must have been especially good from the north, where the valley is. For seen from there, three large temples dominated the rising ground of the city; behind them ran the still higher circuit of the city wall. The position of the temple in the old city is equally striking, though in a different way (plate 13b). Rising ground, which was naturally available in the new city, here had to be created artificially. The ground originally had some spurs of bedrock; a massive terrace was built on these with compactly set boulders; and on this terrace, the temple was erected. While not so steep to the south and west, it stands out all the more to the east and north, where the residential district came closest.

All five temples of Hattusha unmistakably represent a uniform type, although they vary in details (figs. 13, 14). Common features are: the entrance portal at the front, nearly always lying in the axis of the courtyard; pillared halls along the courtyard at least on one side; the location of the adyton at the back, not directly accessible from the court nor in line with the axis of the entrance portal and the court, but shifted sideways. Moreover, the individual rooms are not related to the court, but are arranged in groups which receive light from outside windows. Even the adyton thus lay in broad daylight. The portal, the courtyard, and the adyton are, therefore, the basic elements, while the other parts could be designed more freely. Accordingly, Temple I, for instance, and also, to a certain extent, Temple V, have straight façades, whereas the others have notably restless, offset exteriors. That is an inheritance of Old Anatolian architecture, samples of which we have already seen. In other respects, too, it seems to me, these monumental buildings are thoroughly within the local architectural tradition. The main architectural component of the temple, the unit including the adyton, is still nearly autonomous in Temple I and stands by itself, perhaps an indication of the greater age of this sanctuary. In the other cult buildings, this unit is—more or less in Temple V and completely in Temples II-IV—incorporated into the temple itself. However, this particular unit, which means the nucleus of the cult building, is in layout and arrangement reminiscent of the architecture of the first period of the city. The "House of the God" therefore appears to adhere fundamentally to the old conceptions, although on a monumental scale and with the addition of the propylon, the court and the pillared halls. Unfortunately, we are unable as yet to corroborate this assumption either in Hattusha or in any other site in Hittite territory from the evidence of older cult buildings. There is not

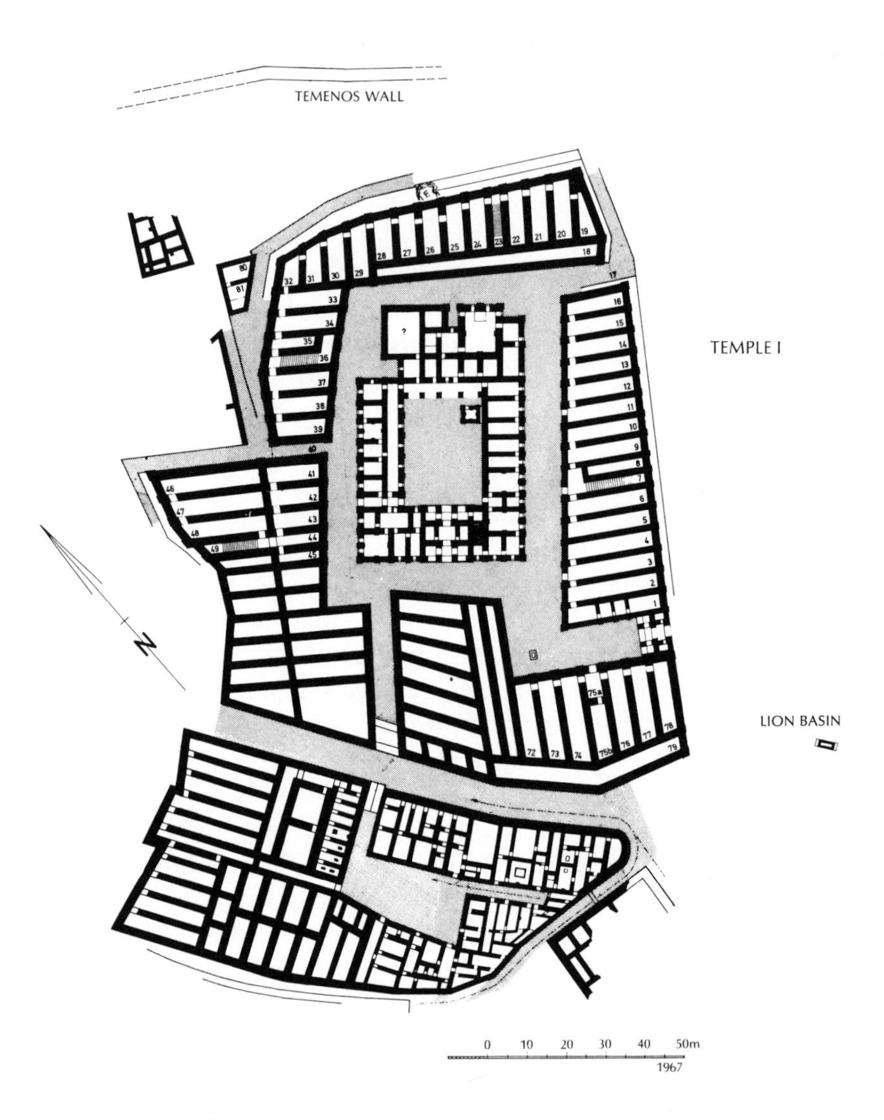

Figure 13. Plan of Temple I

a single building from Old Hittite or even pre-Hittite times in Central Anatolia known to have served unquestionably as a temple.

We said "House of the God," but the question arises: of which god or gods? Temple V in the upper city with its two adyta, each with a base for the cult-statue, was probably a double temple of two deities. But neither here nor in any of the other temples do we have an indication as to the identity of the gods in question. The large temple in the lower city, a huge building surrounded on all sides by storage rooms and situated in a precinct of its own, separated from the rest of the lower city by a wall with a gate, may have been the temple of the Weather God of Hatti. This is suggested by clay tablets found in its eastern storerooms in 1962. If so, this may also have been a double temple, for one of the tablets contains the following text:

> "Weather God of Heaven and Sun Goddess of Arinna: the gold and silver reserve has been examined. The deity has now been made as a statue in silver covered with gold in the shape of a bull standing on all fours. Two new temples in a building-complex for the Weather God of Heaven and the Sun Goddess of Arinna have been built."

If Temple I was that of the Weather God of Hatti, does the temple of the Sun Goddess of Arinna lie westward of it, but in the same *temenos*, where some storerooms already excavated, separated from the eastern complex by a road, were probably part of a second sacred building? Excavations started in this area in the summer of 1967 will furnish further evidence.

Due to the very uneven ground, secular building in the upper part of the city was not dense. There were mostly single houses, the more pretentious ones standing on specially erected terraces. On the northern, more level terrain, however, houses were crowded in close to one another—an architectural characteristic of oriental towns of all times. Part of a residential quarter has been excavated there which is separated from the sacred precinct of Temple I by a heavy double wall, partly buttressed. Here, too, the houses are thoroughly in the Old Anatolian tradition, but they are built in

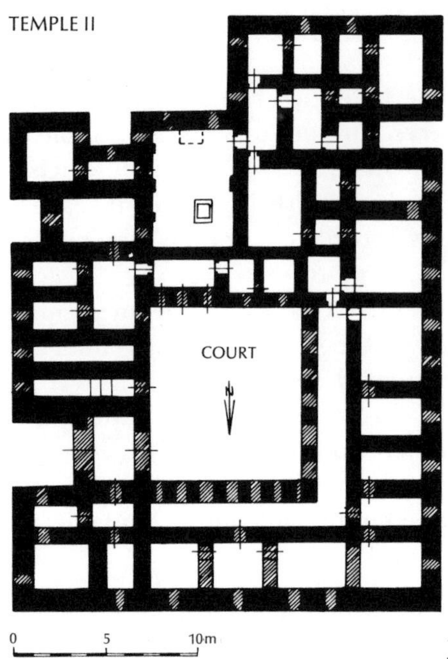

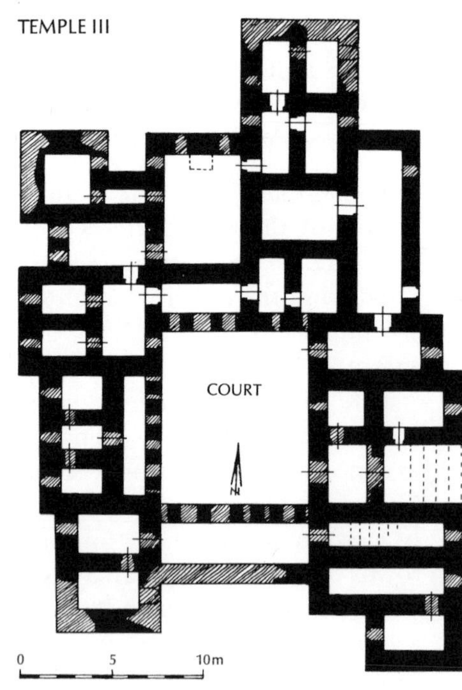

Figure 14. Plans of temples II-V

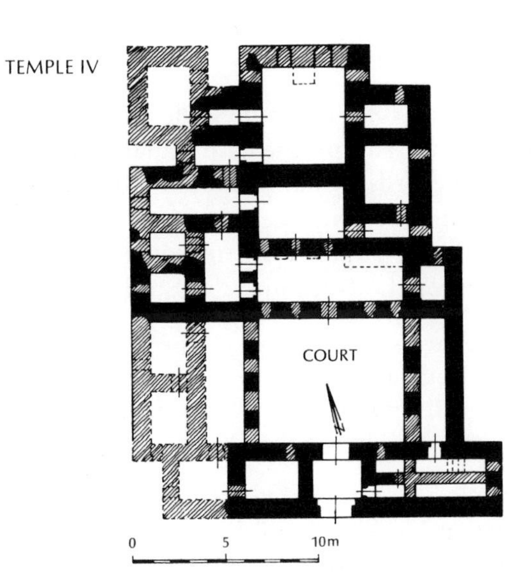
TEMPLE IV
COURT
0
5
10m

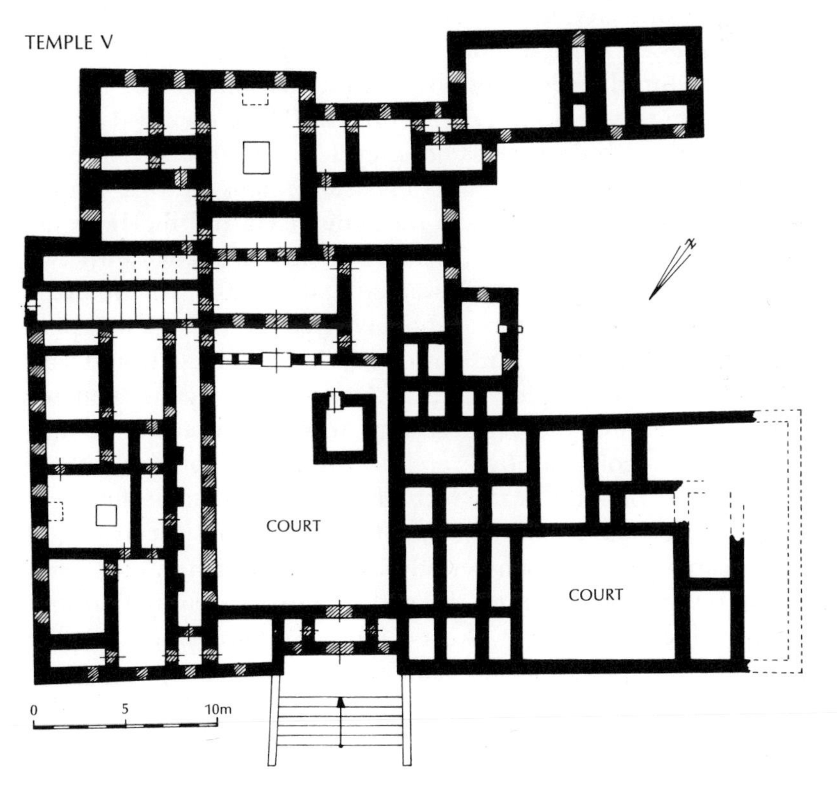
TEMPLE V
COURT
COURT
0
5
10m

blocks so closely together that sometimes the outer walls touch, making it difficult to differentiate the individual premises. If we had private and legal records, so far almost totally lacking, there would probably be plenty of evidence for quarrels over property. We have, instead, a hint of another urgent concern in the abovementioned instruction for the Hazannu, the Burgomaster. It says:

> "Furthermore, the overseer, who is up there in Hattusha, when he calls the watchmen to the look-out, cries out at the first nightwatch: Extinguish the fire! And at the middle nightwatch he cries out: The fire shall be guarded!"

The danger of fire was ubiquitous because of the copious use of wood in monumental and ordinary buildings.

The exact dating of monumental buildings or even individual districts of the city still raises great difficulties and has not as yet progressed beyond more or less well-founded assumptions. The lack of building inscriptions and foundation records is most regrettable in this respect. Levels IVb and IVa of the royal citadel belong to the 14th century as does level 2 of the northern lower city with the large Temple I. The storerooms of this temple underwent partial alterations in the time of Hattushili III in the first half of the 13th century. Level III of the citadel with two sublevels, and level 1 of the lower city, also with two sublevels, are dated to the 13th century, probably after 1280 B.C. The upper city may not have been built until this time, which would also apply to the four temples in its territory. We would then see them as creations of the 13th century, an assumption not at variance with the typology of their architecture. Here, however, there is no certainty because of the lack of absolutely datable finds. It is, on the other hand, an established fact that the city at its largest as it appeared in the fourth period of its history, maintained itself without retrenchments until the end of Hittite domination and the fall of the court of the Great Kings. The great hieroglyphic inscription at Nişantaş (plate 14a) in the southern upper city is not of Shuppiluliuma I, as had been erroneously believed until a few years ago, but of the second Great King of that name, the last

A

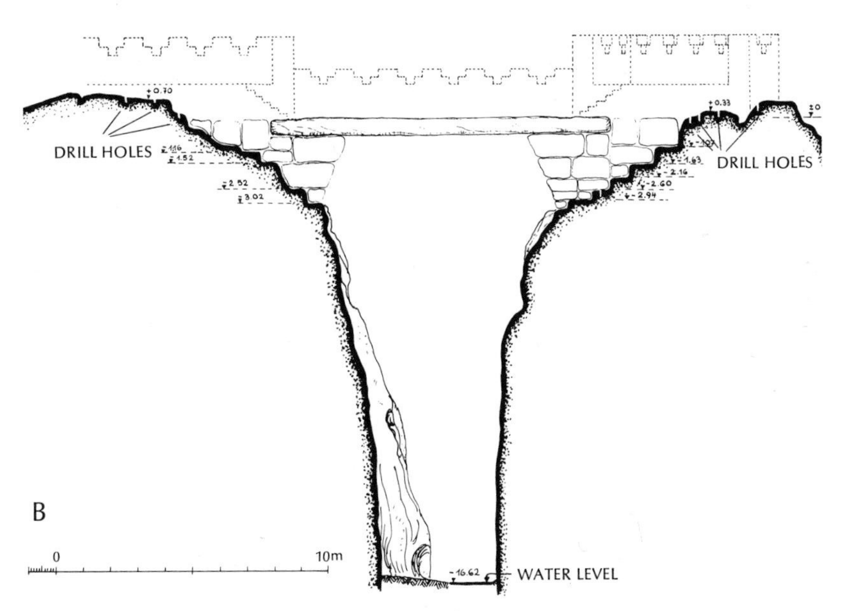

Figure 15. Bridge across Büyükkaya-deresi
A. reconstruction. B. section

Hittite king known to us who ruled around 1200 B.C. or shortly after. At this time, building was evidently still continuing in Hattusha, for besides the rock inscription, there are on Nişantepe the remains of a large structure certainly going back to the time of the same Great King. Yet another much more ambitious undertaking was in progress at that time. It was presumably in the 13th century that the rocky mountain called Büyükkaya, situated east of the city and east of the deep gorge, was incorporated into the city area by means of connecting walls which crossed the gorge twice, on the north and south sides, in an engineering feat still impressive today (fig. 15). The builders went on to connect this Büyükkaya with the northernmost tip of the old city by a far flung and laborious wall-circuit, incorporating yet another area into the city. The high rampart which was to have carried the fortification wall had proceeded to a little over half its intended length when the city perished and its existence came to an abrupt end. This event, the fall of the Hittite capital, will have to be discussed in more detail when we turn our attention to the citadel and the palace of the Hittite Great Kings of the 14th and 13th centuries B.C.

III

HATTUSHA. THE ROYAL FORTRESS OF THE 14TH AND 13TH CENTURIES B.C.

Nowhere in the numerous documents from the Hittite archives do we find clues to the exact appearance of the palace of the Great Kings of the Hittite Empire. The "palace" is, however, a concept which frequently occurs in the texts in an architectural as well as an economic sense, that is, both as the residence of the kings and the center of political and economic life. The "palace" likewise appears as the greatest and most influential landowner. This is not surprising in an empire in which the monarch, as the head of the state in all its manifold functions, and the state itself did not yet represent separate concepts.

Palaces of the Great Kings existed not only in the capital but also elsewhere in the country. They were occupied by the king when he was traveling in order to fulfill his religious obligations and visited the great sanctuaries of the empire. We should, perhaps, not expect too much of these palaces with respect to their size and architectural form. Often they may have been no more than what one might call royal villas. It is not unlikely that a villa of this kind is indicated in a land-deed stating that a "house" of the city of Hattusha in Sharishsha has been invested with landed property. More pretentious, perhaps, were the houses in which the Great Kings used to stay during the winter recess, when the court was not residing in Hattusha. Murshili II (1333-1305), for instance, is known to have passed the winter repeatedly in other towns of the Hatti-land, such as Ankuwa and Marashantiya. However, we know nothing about the remains of either of these or of palaces elsewhere.

There must have been more than one palace in Hattusha itself, since there is an incidental reference to a "palace of the grandfather" in connection with the capital. This could mean the palace of a forebear of the reigning king who is, unfortunately, not identified in the text in question. This example is probably not even an isolated instance. It is conceivable that certain buildings in Boğazköy, parts of which are still visible in ruins, such as Sarıkale, Yenicekale, and also the so-called south fortress, should be identified as palaces of this kind. This question will possibly be settled by future investigations.

Although extensive literary evidence concerning the palaces and their appearance is lacking, there are, nonetheless, some documents from which we can draw inferences and gain at least some insight into the functions of the residential court of the Great Kings. There is, for example, an instruction for the palace personnel concerning the regulations for the purification of the food, drink, and clothing of the Great Kings. It acquaints us with a great number of palace servants. More comprehensive and more important to us, however, is the so-called MESHEDI-text. It is the protocol of the guard or the bodyguard—if this translates the concept correctly, which it would seem to from the various contexts. Of the text, with the colophon "Instruction for the Bodyguard," unfortunately only the first tablet is preserved. Linguistic criteria would date the text to the latter period of the empire, presumably the second half of the 13th century B.C. The instructions are generally binding and not limited to a certain palace, nor even restricted to the capital itself. This is evident from a passage stating: "The bodyguards step aside to the right during the . . . to the *arkiu*-house. If, however, in any town it is impossible to step to the right, they step to the left." Yet in spite of these qualifications, the MESHEDI-text is of a considerable significance. First, because it tells us about the size and about at least some of the inhabitants of a royal residence. Second, because in its details it suggests architectural arrangements which are not too dissimilar from what has actually been found in Hattusha. The regulations of the MESHEDI-text may therefore also have been binding for the palace of the capital.

Among the personnel there appear washermen, doormen, grooms, members of the bodyguard with various ranks, the guard, pages with their superior, a barber, a doctor, a chamberlain, a reciter of prayers, the Hazannu (the Burgomaster) who accompanies the king together with others when he drives out in his chariot. In the palace there are the following practical installations: a dairy, a kitchen, a toilet, and a pantry; and the following architectural elements (restricted here to those affected by the functions of the MESHEDI): a large gate, a gate-house in front of which the guard is posted. The doorman has his station in the gate-house, which also has a side entrance. To the rear is the court of the bodyguards, where during the royal ceremonies the MESHEDI are lined up on one side and the pages on the other. Adjoining this court of the bodyguard is a building also with a court called the halentuwa-house. Its occupants are the king and the queen. From descriptions of halentuwa-houses given elsewhere, these are known to have had windows whose curtains were drawn up in the morning; they contained a throne, an offering table, and a hearth. In this particular case we may see the halentuwa-house as part of the residential palace. The king emerges from the halentuwa-house to perform official functions, and, at the end of the ceremony, he enters it again. In some unexplained connection with the palace buildings, the MESHEDI-text also mentions an altar at which the bodyguard worships the tutelary god of the lance. In addition, there appears an *E-arkiu,* that is, an *arkiu*-house, probably a part of a cult building. Furthermore, we hear of a house of the GAL MESHEDI, that is, of the great MESHEDI, a rank frequently held by royal princes, for example, by Zida, the brother of Shuppiluliuma I and later by Hattushili III and Tuthaliya IV during their father's lifetime. From the context, it is impossible to judge whether this house was an integral part of the palace in its wider sense or if it stood apart from it. In any case, from this incomplete survey of the MESHEDI-text, which is incidentally in need of a thorough study, we learn that there were Hittite palace buildings in the 13th century which, with regard to the number and functions of their occupants, and to the number of their gates, courts, and structures, far exceeded what could be accommodated in a single residential building. This was a whole palace district with functionally arranged wings and subdivisions. The notion of a seraglio resembling the courts of the Ottoman Padishahs would, I think, roughly—only roughly, though—correspond to the architectural setting of the regulations and actions described in the MESHEDI-text. The only palace building recovered by the excavations in Hattusha seems to answer this description fairly well.

Büyükkale, the "Great Fortress," as it is called today, was already in the pre-Hittite age at the beginning of the second millennium B.C. a favored point within the city of Hattush, and continued to be so in the Hittite city Hattusha. This citadel, if we are not msitaken, always remained the dynastic center of the community. This did not change with the coming of the Hittite Empire, not even when during this period the city expanded far to the south. At that time, Büyükkale, the highest point and an integral part of the old city, lost its physically predominant position, since the new city rose considerably above the citadel. The continued use of the old mountain for the royal residence is surely an expression of conservatism, of adherence to old traditions.

The rocky base on which its stands makes Büyükkale a natural stronghold (plate 14b). This is especially so on the east and north sides. Steep precipices and towering groups of rocks, some of them rising almost vertically from the valley and the gorge, make the north and east sides of the mountain almost unscalable. The west and south sides have considerably gentler slopes, so these had to be built up. The evidence of the excavations assigns the beginning of this extensive engineering process to the older phase of the Hittite Empire, to the fourth period of the history of Hattusha. To this period belongs levels IVb3-b1, IVa and IIIb-a of the Hittite fortress of the 14th and 13th centuries. The beginning of IVb3 was at about the turn from the 15th to the 14th century, while the latest level, IIIa, belongs to the later 13th century and lasts to the end of the Hittite capital. What dates we can fix accurately within this short period of scarcely two centuries will have to be discussed later.

Little has survived of the royal fortress of the older phase of this period which includes levels IVb-3-IVa. Destructions caused by fire and, in an even higher degree, intentional demolitions in the course of later building have left very little of the architectural structures (fig. 16). The fortress was at that time surrounded by fortifications on its south, west, and north sides which connected with the city-wall at both ends. A gate with a small forecourt and a wide, nearly rectangular gate-chamber led into the interior (fig. 17). This gate with its two sets of doors and a chamber slightly set back within the curtain-walls represents a type one would not expect to find in such an early period. Most of its counterparts—at Arslantepe, Carchemish, and also at some North Syrian sites—belong to the early first millennium B.C. However, on the basis of careful investigations of the foundations, foundation trenches, and their contents, and by the structural connection with the city wall, it has been proved beyond doubt that the Büyükkale gate belongs to level IVb2 and therefore no later than the middle of the 14th century B.C.

During this whole period the lower plateau of the acropolis was covered with mostly smaller buildings many of which were replaced suprisingly quickly. From their remaining ground plans (fig. 18) it appears that they represent a type of house which corresponds in contour and layout to the Central Anatolian tradi-

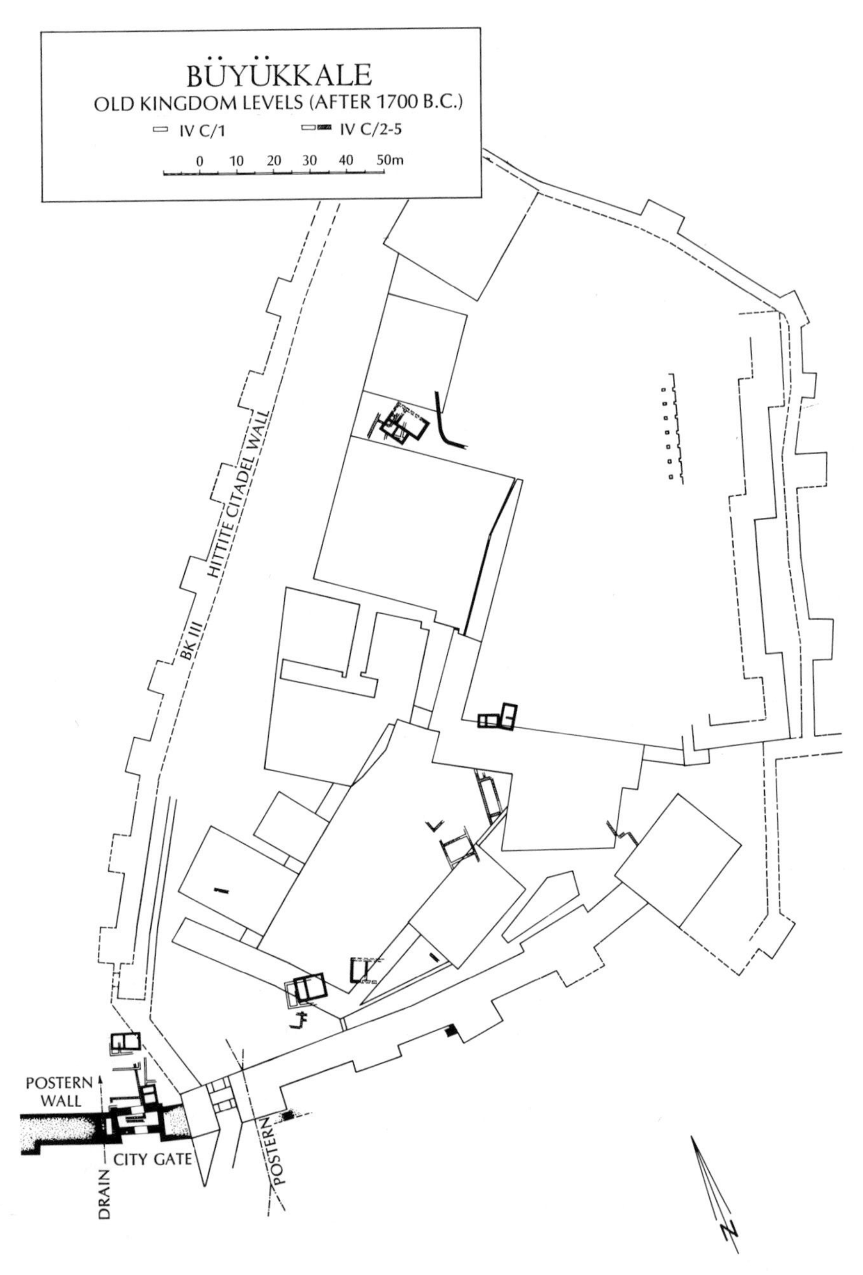

Figure 16. Early Büyükkale:
A. Old Kingdom levels

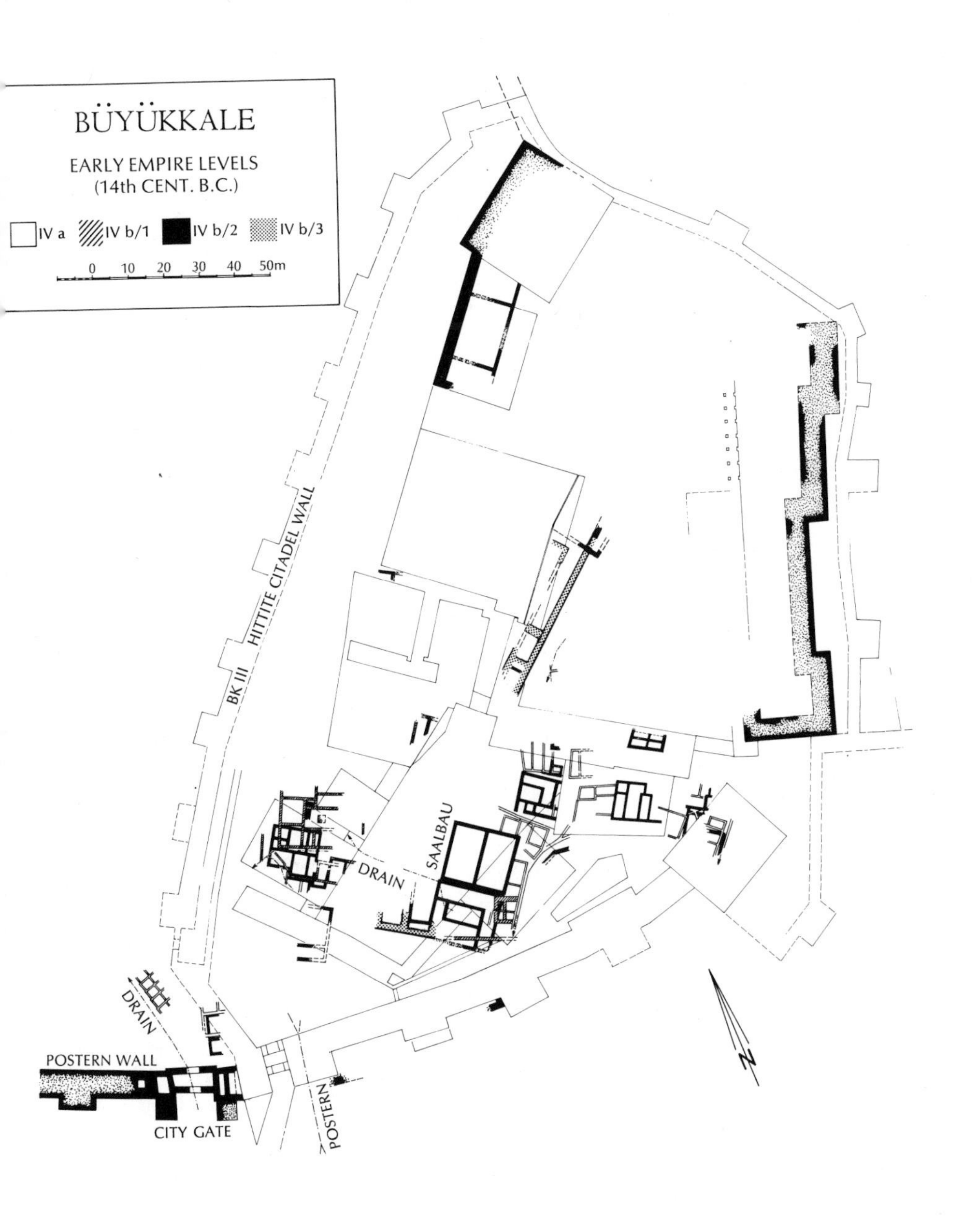

B. Early Empire levels

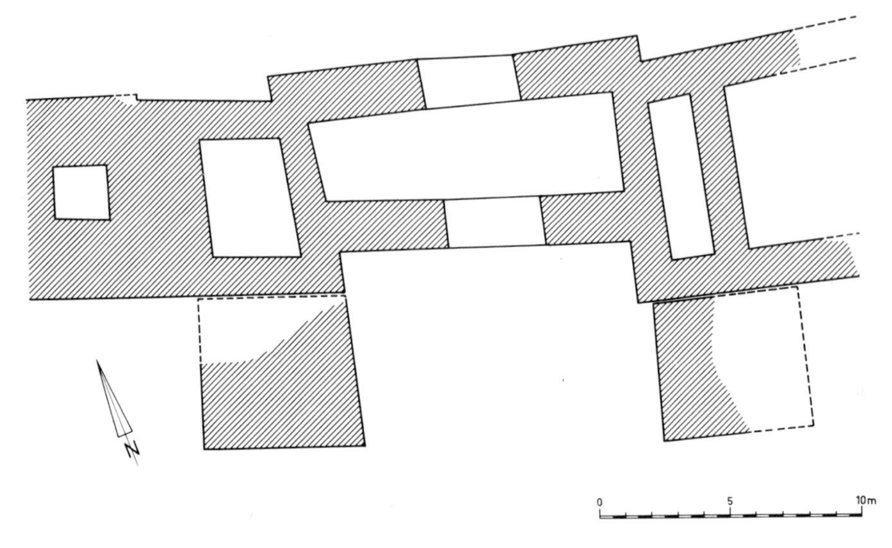

Figure 17. Gate of Büyükkale level IVb2

tion which in Hattusha proper can be traced back at least to the beginning of the second millennium B.C. They are all freestanding houses. Despite the incompleteness of the remains, the orientation in levels IVb3 to IVa is noticeably consistent, approximately southeast-northwest and northeast-southwest. Only two buildings in this part of the fortress are conspicuous for their size and the dimensions of their rooms. The northernmost building consists of only two long rooms parallel to each other. One of them, 14.60 meters long and almost 8 meters wide, is the largest room so far discovered at Boğazköy. The entrance to this building was in the center of the long west side; the rooms therefore were wide rather than deep; the front room had a pavement and was probably a vestibule. The second building stands directly to the south, nearly wall to wall with the first, although completely detached. Its over-all dimensions are at least as large as the first but the plan consists of at least three, if not four, rooms. The central room, measuring 4.20 by 9.50 meters, is nearly rectangular. It is prominent in the plan but it lay about 1.30 meters below the

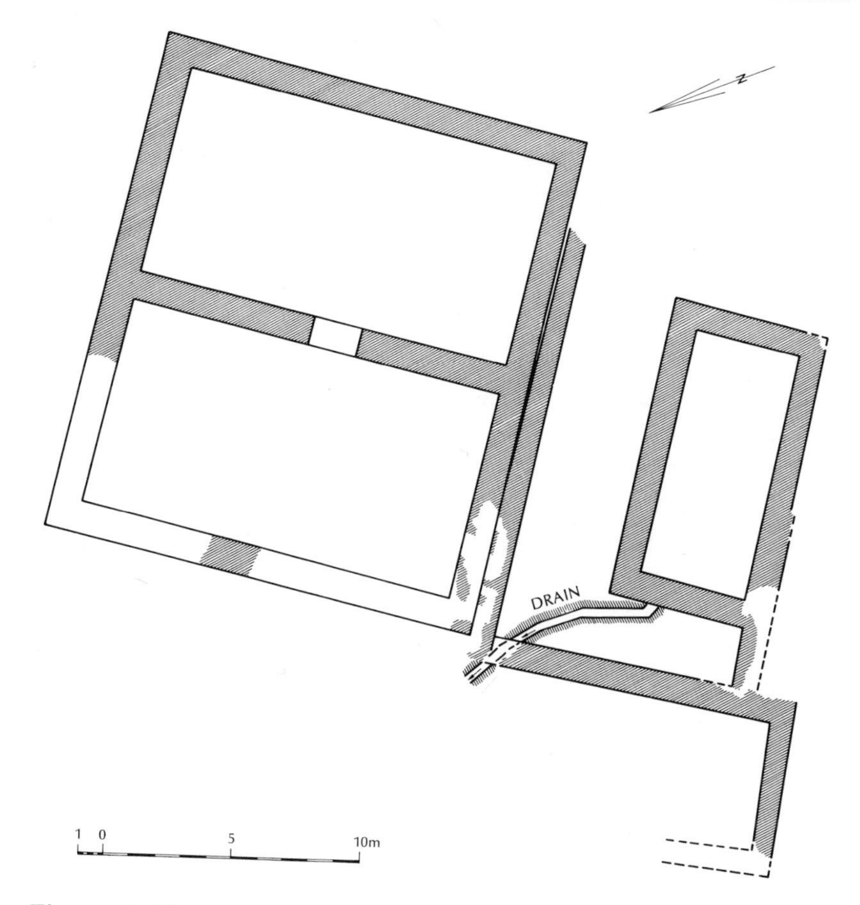

Figure 18. House plans of Büyükkale level IVb

ground level like a cellar. On its hard clay floor there was a thin fugitive whitish to yellow layer, with the impressions of interwoven vegetable fibers: the remains of rush mats which had covered the floor. Level with the floor is the inlet of a stone-built channel, which leaves the building in the northernmost corner. In this central room we found a large painted vessel in the shape of a duck, reminiscent of Aegean *askos* forms. It is conceivable that the two buildings just described, which stand out so conspicuously against their surroundings, served ritual rather than secular purposes and were, in fact, small chapels. Of the superstructure, unfortunately, so little is preserved that it is of no help in determining the original purpose of the two buildings. But in the debris of the northern building, we found six limestone cubes measuring *c.* 10 by 7.5-9 centimeters. Four of them were originally white, two had been painted black on one side. Five of them have a drill hole 1.4 centimeters in diameter and 2.5 centimeters deep in one side. Their shape, number, and size make an architectural use unlikely. They were probably used as decorative elements on the base of an altar or a statue, although there is no strict proof for this.

Another discovery suggests that this part of the fortress was not used simply for secular purposes in the period in question. It was made in 1963 in level IVb2 next to a building of this period not quite 30 meters to the west of the houses just described. In a cache, together wtih three red burnished pitchers, lay two bulls almost 90 centimeters in height (plates 15, 16). They are made of clay and covered with a light red to red, highly polished slip, with special areas of their bodies painted cream: patches on the shoulders and the haunches, the triangle on the foreheads and the inner parts of the lyre-shaped horns. Their white eyes are inlaid with black pupils. Each bull is bridled around its neck by a white-painted halter, attached to a ring which passes through its nostrils. Each bull has a funnel-shaped opening at the nape of the neck for pouring in liquids and two openings in the nostrils serving as outlets. The bulls were obviously little statues as well as cult-vessels into which, or out of which, libations were poured on certain occasions. However, they are not just two ordinary bulls but rather a team of two special bulls. This is evident not only because they were found lying together *in situ* but also because they are made as counterparts: the tail of one of them hangs down its left leg and that of the other down its right leg to just above the hoof. They were evidently meant to stand side by side. There was in Hittite cult only one team of sacred bulls: Sheri and Hurri, the bulls of the Weather God, whose names mean "Day" and "Night" in Hurrian, who pull the chariot of the Weather God and also appear before him and other gods to plead for one who says a prayer.

> Sherish, my lord, bull, you who appear before the Weather God of Hatti-land! My prayer which has to be said in this matter convey to the gods so that the gods, the lords, the gods of heaven and the underworld, hear these words.

Although these two large bull statuettes do not have characteristic divine attributes like the conical caps Sheri and Hurri wear in the rock reliefs of Yazılıkaya, I am nonetheless inclined to see them as the team of bulls of the Weather God. Fragments of such large-scale terra-cotta sculptures have been found in several places in Hattusha, including the northern residential area. This seems natural if we keep in mind that these bull-shaped divine beings interceded for humans with the higher gods, and should be thought of as helpers-in-need not only in special cult buildings but also at home and at the hearth.

In contrast to the lower terrace of the citadel, the upper area is known to have been covered by much more extensive and monumental buildings at the time of levels IVb3 and IVb2. What little has survived is sufficient for a reconstruction of the essential elements. Along the northern part of the east and west sides, huge terraces of cyclopean boulders were erected to enlarge the area available for construction. These terraces served as the substructures of large buildings. On the west side, we have the remnants of at least three rooms of such a terrace building, destroyed in a conflagration. In the interior of the citadel the foundations of a very long wall remain *in situ,* met at right angles by somewhat thinner cross-walls. A comparison with later structures, to be discussed presently, suggests that they are most likely the foundation of a colonnade opening towards a court and provided with a series of rooms at the back. This is an architectural feature which belongs to the basic elements of Hittite architecture of the Imperial age. Although little survives of the citadel buildings of levels IVb3 to IVa, the upper terrace evidently was occupied by the main complex of monumental buildings, while the lower was covered with smaller structures and houses. We may assume that the palace proper stood on the upper level and that the lower one was occupied by the lower echelons of the court. This latter district was, understandably, subject to more rapid changes and intensive alterations than the more permanent institutions of the upper terrace. The buildings on the lower terrace in level IVa, the latest phase of the period just discussed, are of a remarkably modest appearance. They differ strangely from their immediate predecessors of IVb1 or, for that matter, IVb2 in their much simpler technical execution. They have no signs of violent interference, whereas the previous structures all bear unmistakable traces of destruction. The question arises whether and how these observations can be reconciled with the literary tradition of the city of Hattusha discussed in Chapter I. We shall return to this problem presently. But first the royal citadel of levels IIIb and IIIa will have to be dealt with. It is very different, but also more extensive, for much more has been preserved, in spite of heavy destruction and sad losses.

The entire surface of the acropolis, both its upper and lower terraces, are now occupied by a coherent palace complex made up of a great number of interrelated structures. This is the seraglio we postulated at the beginning of this chapter on the strength of the MESHEDI-text. It was not created in a single building operation but was rather the outcome of three-quarters of a century of building. The situation is best understood by starting with the latest phase of the palace as it existed under the last Great Kings who resided in Hattusha.

The citadel is now surrounded on all sides by fortifications, including the hitherto open west side which faces the lower city (figs. 19, 20; plate 17a). The new citadel separated the king from his profane surroundings to a much greater extent than had previously been the case. It is not improbable that this was the expression of a development which is perceptible at the beginning of the Hittite Empire and which became pronounced during the 13th century B.C. Hittite kingship came increasingly closer to ancient oriental concepts. Theocracy entered the idea of kingship. The

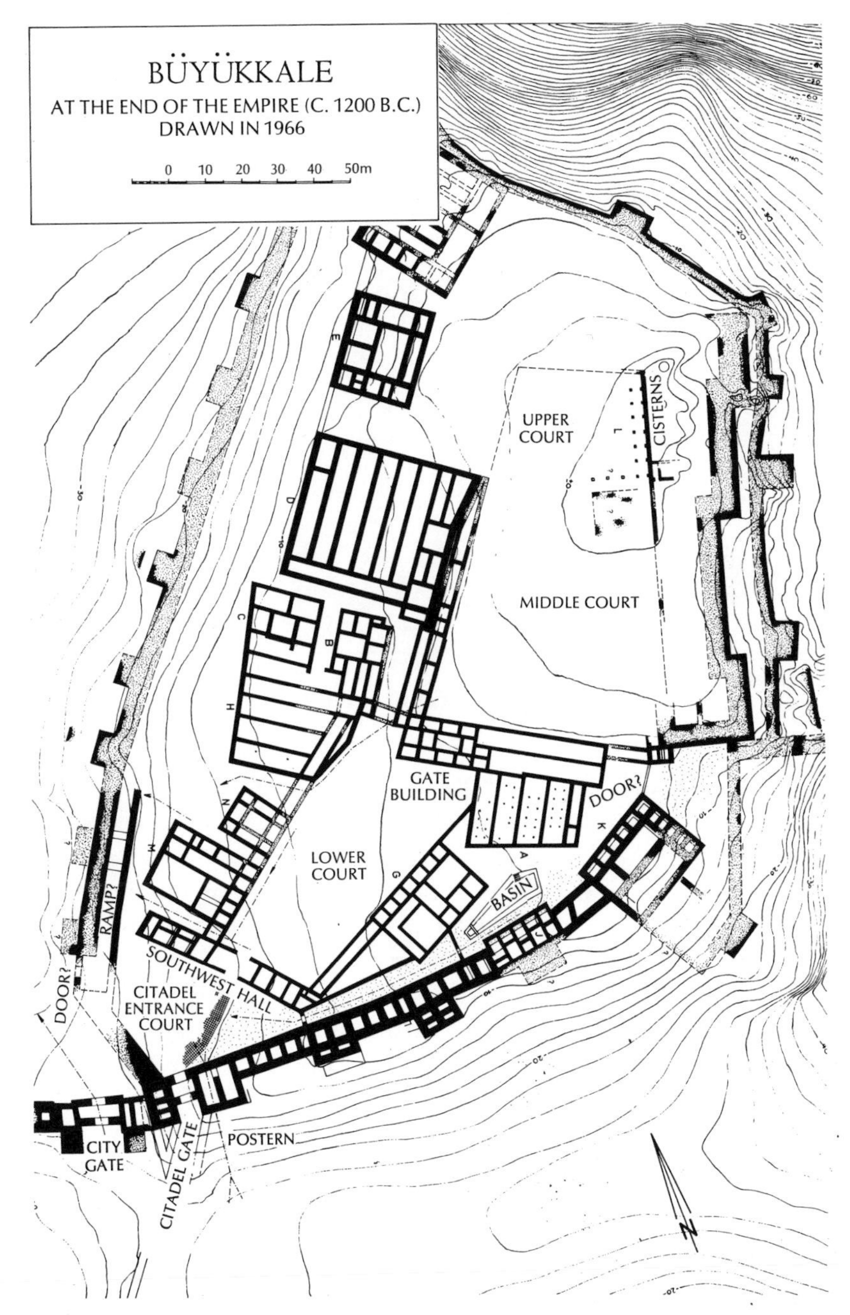

Figure 19. Büyükkale, general plan of 13th century B.C.

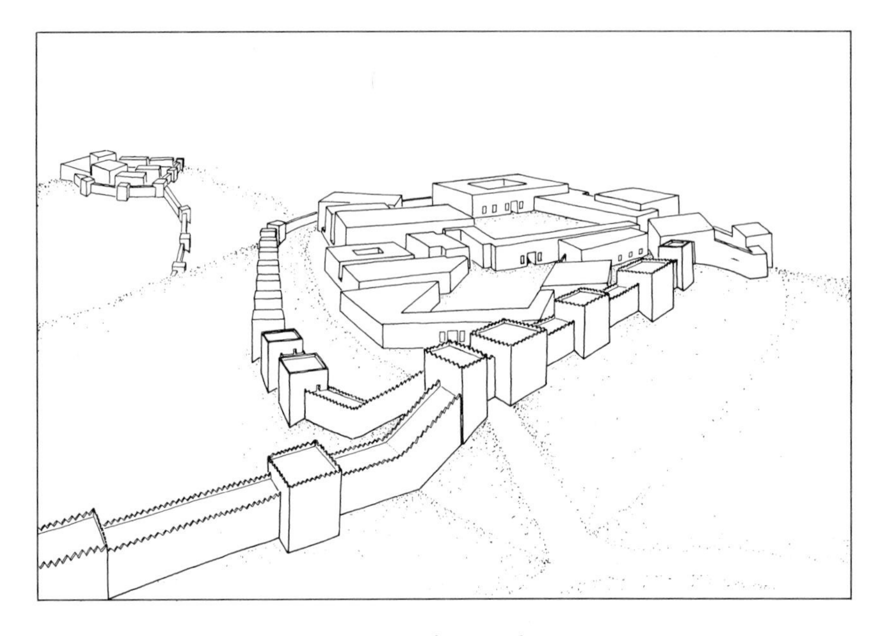

Figure 20. Büyükkale. Reconstruction, 13th century B.C.

king's status now required that he must stand aloof from the ordinary people and communicate with them only under special safeguards.

The enclosure wall of the citadel was, however, not merely a dividing line, but a fortification with heavy curtain walls, nearly 9 meters thick on the south side in a casemate system, provided with towers and bastions which made it fully defensible. To have a maximum of building space within the citadel, the new level retained the terraces at the edges of the upper plateau which had been built during the previous periods (Büyükkale levels IVb3-IVa). Accordingly, the fortification wall runs farther below along the very steep and rocky slopes. The planning and engineering of this wall line command respect for the Hittite builders.

The interior of this externally protected and isolated citadel now became one single, great palace area. In the previous period the lower terrace was still covered with relatively small buildings, incoherent in spacing and without any recognizable orientation. We now find a complex dominated almost exclusively by monumental buildings, worthy of the name royal seraglio in the full sense of the term. Admittedly, not all of the buildings which made up this complex survived and could be recovered by the excavations of the citadel which were concluded in the autumn of 1965. At the highest point in the east and north part of the upper terrace, we see nothing but the naked rock. The buildings which once stood on this spot were almost completely demolished, and their elements were reused elsewhere in the post-Hittite period. Notwithstanding the gaps, enough remains of the palace to give a clear idea of its fundamental features and to allow a reconstruction even of some of its details. What have been recovered by the excavations are of course mainly the foundations, or, at best, the lower storeys of units which in general must have been several storeys high.

There were three entrances to the palace district. One of them is very well preserved and accessible again today; the exact location and function of the second is not yet clearly understood; but the existence of a third entrance is clear from the preserved remains. The two main gates were in the southwest and southeast corners of the fortress. Its site is approximately trapezoidal, with a maximum length of 250 meters and width of 150 meters. Owing to the lie of the ground the ascent was easiest at the south side. The southwest gate was reached via a rather steep artificial ramp which was suitable for walking or traffic in sedan-chairs only, not for chariots. The gate itself resembles the southern city-gates of the so-called new city, with two doorways and a fairly wide forecourt between two flanking towers. At a much lower level, the old city wall with its own gate links up with the fortress wall. Of the gate at the southeast corner, only the large outer court, parts of the flanking walls, and the inner passage are preserved. This is very regrettable, since these traces suggest that it was a gate structure of individual character, unparalleled in contemporary Hittite architecture. Unlike the more conventional southwest gate, it seems to have been designed to suit the nature of the (here particularly uneven) ground. The disadvantage of the terrain had to be overcome since only here, in the depression adjacent to the southern part of the acropolis, was it feasible to construct a ramp rising evenly and with a gradient suitable for chariots. At the southwest gate the presence of the adjoining old city wall and the road leading directly upward to the new city prevented the planning of so spacious a construction. There is, therefore, hardly any doubt that the southeast gate at least equaled the southwest gate in importance as a main entrance to the citadel. There is, finally, a third entrance in the south part of the western citadel wall. It opened to a staircase which led up to the terraces that supported the most prominent buildings of the palace district. This passage accommodated the pedestrian traffic between the fortress and the northern lower city, that is, the old city, and at the same time provided the shortest connection between the citadel and the *temenos* with the sanctuary of the Weather God of Hatti far below in the north. It is, however, unlikely that the king ever used this ascent in the course of official ceremonies.

Now we come to the architectural forms of the interior of the citadel (fig. 21). We notice immediately that what we see is not an architectural layout of a type known elsewhere in identical or related form, but a thoroughly individual architectural design dependent upon the nature of the site and the irregular profile of the rocky hill, leveled with the aid of artificial terraces to serve as building ground. The same is not true of the individual buildings which, combined, constitute the residence of the Great Kings. It is evident that buildings B, C, E, F, G, K, and M in their plan and interior subdivisions follow old traditional building forms of Central Anatolia. In more modest examples we can trace their beginnings back to the early centuries of the second millennium B.C., even in Hattusha proper, as in the previous chapter. But there are other buildings—such as A, D, and H—whose ancestry we do not yet know. We will later consider their original function. All of these structures—the older, traditional group as well as the newly introduced types—consist of free-standing units which are occasionally connected by short walls or narrow, covered passages.

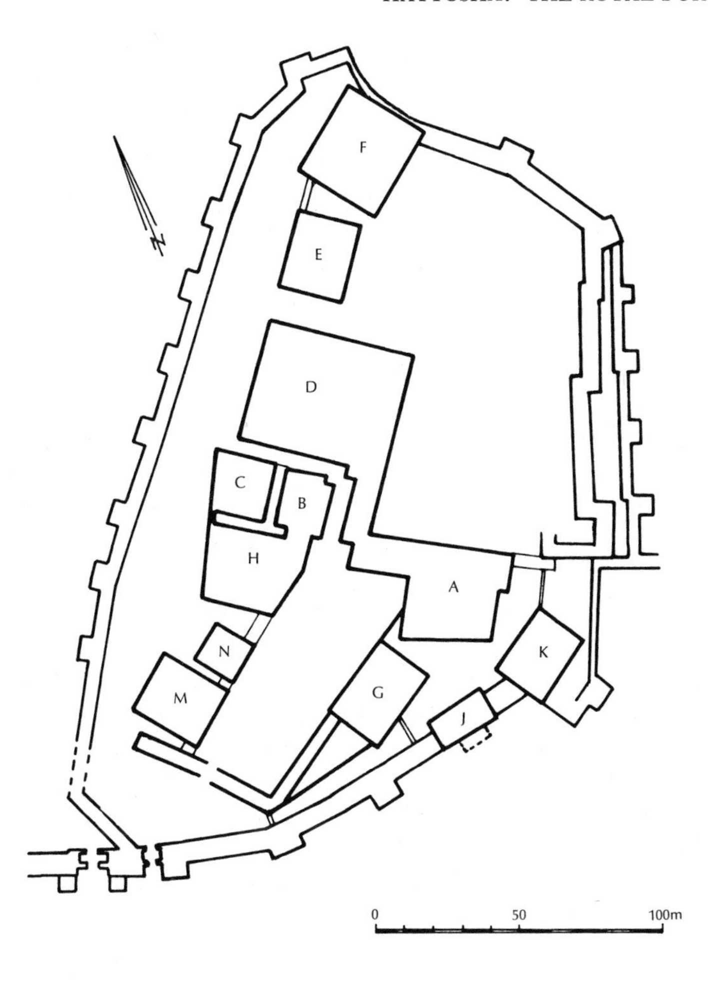

Figure 21. Schematic plan of Büyükkale with letters designating individual buildings

This kind of connection is deceptive, however, for these very passages, of which only the foundations remain, prove upon closer examination to have a special function of their own, thus emphasizing the autonomy of each structure of the citadel. And yet, the individual buildings are all subordinate to a larger concept and are integrated by the courtyards.

Four of these courts, beginning at the lowest point near the southwest gate and succeeding each other up to the summit in the northeast, represent the axis of the palace district to which everything else is related. Unfortunately, we do not know their original names. Designations such as citadel entrance court and lower, middle, and upper courtyard are merely topographical nicknames. The courtyards, though they differed from one another in size and contour, have one thing in common: they were bordered on more than one side by open colonnades. In the upper courtyard, the beddings for the bases of the pillars of colonnades are preserved on two sides. In the middle courtyard, the long, narrow foundations along the south and west sides also indicate colonnades. The reconstruction is obvious, for the findings correspond to those of the lower courtyard where, in the context of building G, heavy limestone bases of pillars were actually found on, and next to, the foundations on the southeast side. The parallelism between the lower and the middle court is corroborated by the corresponding construction of the foundations which served as stylobates to support the rows of pillars.

These large courtyards bordered by open pillar halls lent a distinct architectural flavor, a surprising monumentality, to the residence of the great kings. This was enhanced by the fact that each courtyard was separated from its neighbor by portals and gate structures of varying form and size. So, as one passed through these gates from one courtyard into the next, ever new perspectives presented themselves.

Open pillar halls bordering a courtyard are nothing unusual in the Hittite architecture of these centuries. They occur on one or two sides of the inner courts of Temples I, II, III, IV, and V of Hattusha. A particularly distinct example exists at Hüyük near Alaca, fifteen miles north-northeast of Boğazköy. In all these cases they are only parts of a larger building. But in the Hittite royal citadel, they are independent building elements—the connecting and supporting members, to some extent, of the whole complex. Architecturally effective, they also made functional sense. To this question we now turn.

The lower courtyard is separated from the southwest gate by a long and narrow hall. It has an unmistakable resemblance to the façade of Temple IV in the new city, in type rather than in size. The southwest gate of the citadel and the portal leading through the hall to the lower courtyard are connected by a road covered with bright red marble flagstones. It is tempting to think that this "purple road" was of special significance in the court ceremonies. Once arrived in the lower courtyard, one saw buildings which bordered the court either with their longer side, such as G, or with one of their narrow sides, such as M and N. Their façades had been made an integral part of the colonnades. Buildings G and M were of considerable size and at least two storeys high, since there is good evidence of staircases, especially in G. About the purpose of buildings M, N, and E, we know nothing due to the lack of specific finds.

The gate structure which led from the lower into the middle courtyard is of a considerable size. Although no more than its foundations remain, these are so typical and so closely related to the portals of Temple I and the gate structure of Yazılıkaya that they can be safely reconstructed as a triple gateway with porters' cubicles. Unless we are very much mistaken, this is the architectural form which the Hittites used to call an E-Hilammar. This large gate-house on Büyükkale separated and connected the outer and inner parts of the palace, the public quarters and the secluded part. The inner courtyards, the middle as well as the upper, could also be reached by a direct road via the southeast gate, avoiding the lower courtyard. This road entered the middle courtyard at its southeast corner. This must have been the road used by the Great Kings when they left or returned to the palace by chariot.

Buildings A, D, E, and F are connected with the inner courtyards. Together with the lost constructions on the northern and eastern side of the court they formed the core of the palace. Each one of them is so large that individually it merits the name of a palace. In no case, however, do we have more than the ground floors, whose interior subdivision may not have been repeated on the upper levels. The existence of upper floors can be proved for all four buildings, for their position on the slope makes this inevitable, even in the case of A where it is not so obvious at first glance. One entered these buildings from the upper and middle courtyards directly on the level of the upper floor. The ground floor, which is shown on the plan, was reached by means of staircases, recognizable in buildings D, E, and F. The assumption that E and F were privileged residential quarters within the palace is self-evident; they have a distinguished position in the innermost part of the citadel and from here one has a view which extends miles into the countryside. These are, indeed, royal residences. In the huge building D, at the western end of a narrow passage on the ground floor, we found a large number of stamped clay bullae, about 100 of which bore impressions or partial impressions of the seals of the Great Kings of the 14th and 13th centuries up to the last known reigning dynast. A few of them had, obviously, been attached to consignments of goods, most of them perhaps to wooden tablets which we know served as writing material.

Rudolf Naumann, who has worked with me as an architect in Boğazköy for many years, assumes that the second storey did not repeat the plan of the groundfloor with its parallel magazine-like rooms of equal length (fig. 22). He proposes, rather, one huge square hall, nearly 32 meters long on each side. The partition walls between the rooms on the lower floor would have served as foundations for five rows of five wooden pillars, which would have supprted the ceiling of the second storey, resulting in a spacious and impressive hall with twenty-five pillars. I am convinced, as many others are, that Naumann's interpretation is correct. The assumption that this was the audience hall of the Hittite Great Kings is supported in a sense by a fact which has been observed only very recently. In the left rear corner of the lower courtyard, a door opened into a passage which led behind building B and below the level of the middle courtyard to a side entrance of building D. The upper floor of D could then be reached by a staircase to the vestibule in the façade of the audience

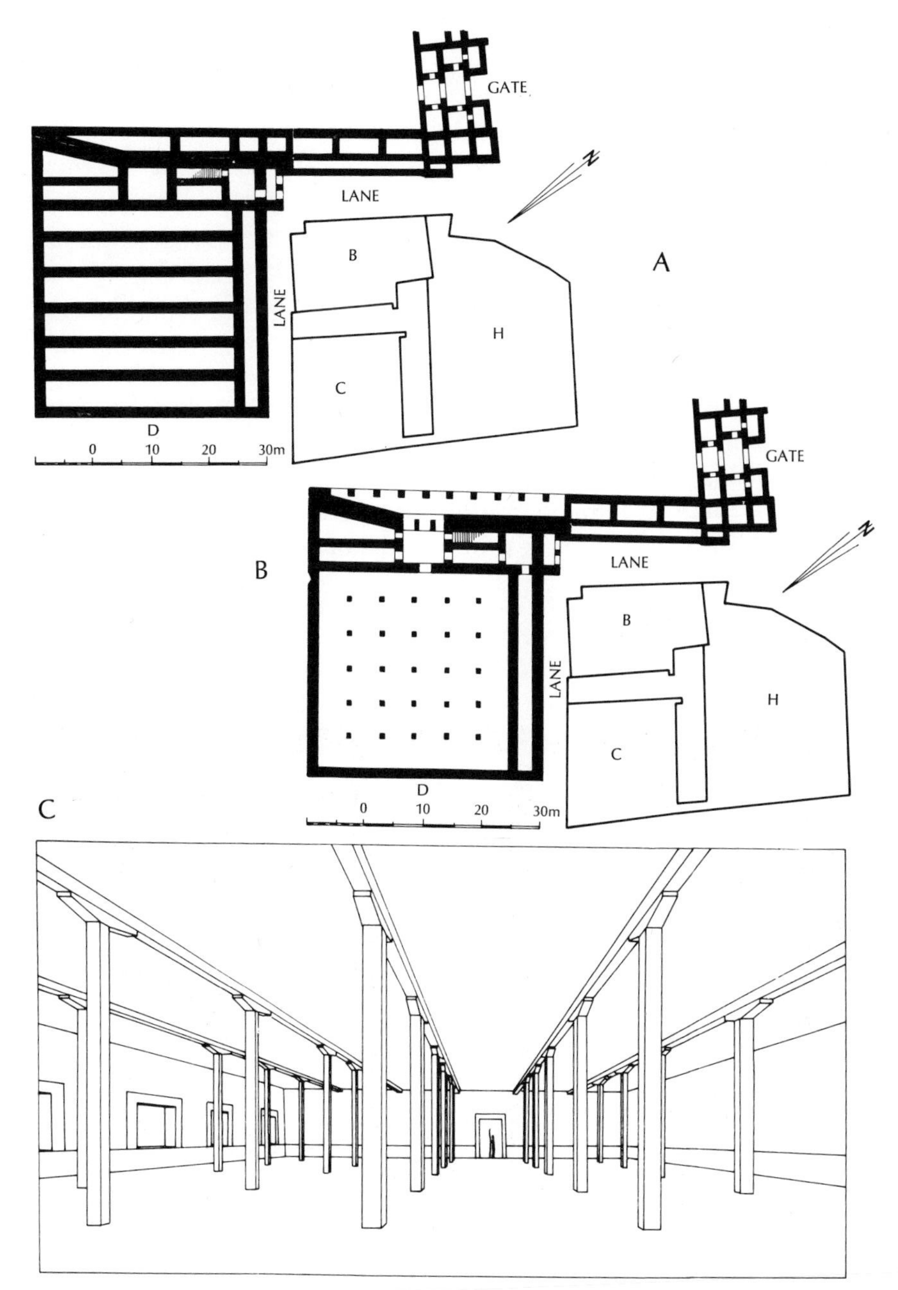

Figure 22. Büyükkale building D with audience hall:
A. ground level. B. upper floor. C. view of interior

hall. We can imagine the Great King entering the audience hall directly from the middle courtyard, the inner court of the more secluded part of the palace. Those who were granted an audience —whether native dignitaries or ambassadors of foreign powers— would make their way from the southwestern gate through the lower courtyard and the passage just mentioned, thus avoiding the inner precincts of the palace. The twofold orientation of this building D, its relation to the inner palace as well as to the outside, would seem to corroborate this interpretation of it as an audience hall.

Building A housed one of the royal archives (fig. 23). A second archive came to light in the ground floor of E. In neither case can it be proved for certain in which storey the tablets were once

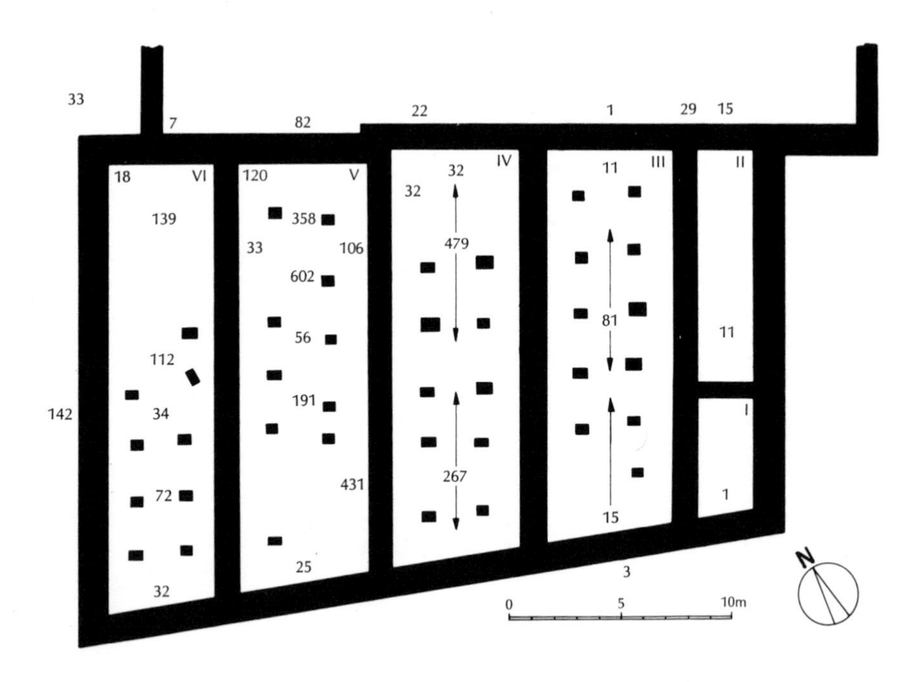

Figure 23. Büyükkale building A: findspots of tablets with numbers to indicate quantities found

kept on their wooden shelves. In A, it is most likely that the library occupied the two central long rooms with two rows of pillars. In building E, the tablets were evidently deposited in the upper floor. When the royal citadel was destroyed and the wooden ceilings went up in flames, the tablets fell into the ground floor and down the adjacent slope of Büyükkale. A third, smaller archive was found in 1957 in the middle room of building K. This archive room and the arrangement and the classification of its documents were described in the first chapter. The distribution of tablets in three locations on the citadel, buildings A, E, and K—perhaps with the exception of the latest texts—may have been due to a reorganization of the library under Tuthaliya IV. They were probably originally all housed in one building; but the building no doubt had to make room for new constructions under this king. We shall return to this later.

C is a building of a very special type. It has only six rooms, five of which surround a central unit. The latter is not strictly square and its walls are constructed of large blocks of limestone tooled on the sides facing the interior of the room. Its floor lies 1.50 meters below that of the surrounding rooms It was found covered with layers of mud and sand which contained numerous small votive vessels and whole nests of imported shells. A small channel forms an outlet at the northern corner. We should think of this room as being open to the sky, without a roof, but with supports on at least two sides of the rooms facing the basin. If I am not mistaken, nothing has as yet been discovered in Hittite architecture which resembles this building. It probably served a ritual purpose. And the long, irregularly shaped basin between buildings A and J (the latter of unusual type, built into the citadel wall) also cannot have been designed for purely practical purposes, unless a people of such strong religious motivation as the Hittites merged the sacred and profane. The basin between A and J has sloping sides neatly lined with limestone. Stairs lead down to the bottom of the basin. Its original west end was later curtailed. Here, too, the interior was filled with mud which yielded a large number of votive vessels, but also large pieces of obsidian, and parts of ivory furniture. This would not suggest an ordinary pond. Furthermore, the shortened south side is exactly the same length as the front of building J, which is close and to which it runs almost parallel. Building and basin seem thus to have formed a unit, the details and purpose of which have to remain uncertain at present.

In spite of some uncertainties, the excavations have yielded a clear general conception of the royal citadel of Hattusha. We purposely began this chapter with the so-called MESHEDI-text. Its buildings, institutions, hierarchy, actions, and ceremonies come to life when one views them against the background of the palace at Büyükkale. As has been emphasized, this text does not explicitly refer to the palace of Hattusha. But I should like to point out that its fits Hattusha quite well, whatever its original frame of reference. The MESHEDI-text, literally taken, also postulates a whole complex of buildings rather than a palace as a single unit. The gate with the porter's lodge, the courtyard of the bodyguard, the gate-house of the halentuwa-house, this house itself, frequented by king and queen, its courtyard—all these descriptions are applicable to the royal residence as recovered at Büyükkale. Also, the other installations like the sanctuary, the storage rooms, kitchen and domestic buildings mentioned in the MESHEDI-text, could easily be accommodated in the excavated area of the citadel. One is tempted to assume that the redactor of the MESHEDI-tablet took his guidelines from the palace of Hattusha.

The MESHEDI-text, as we said before, stands late in the series of Hittite documents, in the second half of the 13th century. It is thus about contemporary with the architectural state of the royal palace just described. This was the final stage. Was the final shape of the palace the result of a great project under one single ruler, or was it erected in gradual stages of expansion? The question must be asked, although the answer is difficult and must remain incomplete.

To the problem of the age of the individual parts a glance at the plan provides an answer: the upper and middle courtyards with the adjoining buildings A, D, E, and F, perhaps also with B and C, form a unit on the basis of their almost identical orientation. The lower courtyard with buildings G, M, N, and the southwest hall look like a more recent annex. Also, this annex presupposes the existence of the southern citadel wall, for the oblique outer wall adjoining G in the southwest is obviously related to these fortifications. The whole annex, in turn, is related to the southwest gate. The paved road along the inside of the fortress wall which connects the southwest gate with the southeast gate and which could be closed at two points by narrow doors, obviously served as a shortcut for the servants of the palace and makes sense only in conjunction with the annex. The annex indeed proved to be stratigraphically later than the inner palace unit at the decisive junctions: building G which is so predominant in the annex is later than A, N is later than M, and M is later than C and H. The doors in the street belong, like the street itself, to the latest phase of the citadel wall. Nor is the basin older than the annex, and building J is even more recent, although still Hittite.

Remembering what has been said about the royal fortress of the 14th century, that is, levels IVb_3 to IVa, an explanation seems readily available: the upper complex is of early origin, but the annex is more recent, and was constructed step by step in the 13th century to add to the palace proper an area which was hitherto only occupied by structures of lesser rank. This interpretation is as correct as it is incorrect. Correct, because the upper district is, in fact, old and the annex later. It is incorrect because what now actually remains of the upper district is, with a few exceptions, hardly older than the annex. It consists mainly of a fundamental reconstruction of buildings which had been destroyed. This fact was quite evident in building D, even more so in F, and especially in A and E. This reconstruction, so far as we can still check the events, retained as much as possible of what previously existed. So we find that the 13th-century palace, both in the traditional older sector and in the so-called annex, was built after a radical destruction of the previously existing palace on the upper plateau of the citadel. Is there evidence to date these events more precisely?

It has been suggested that the temporary transfer of the seat of the court and the government from Hattusha to Dattashsha in the lower country—a change which Muwatalli had intended to be final—proved so detrimental to the capital and its buildings that the old royal citadel fell into ruins. This suggestion never seemed plausible to me, for I cannot imagine that a residence which, after all, harked back several centuries could have been left so utterly without supervision that it was allowed to decay. One must bear in mind that the city of Hattusha as such continued to exist and that the palace certainly did not slip entirely from royal control. Muwatalli himself says of an official called Mittanamuwa, that he "bestowed favor upon him, promoted him and gave him Hattusha." He evidently invested him with the fief of the city when it was no longer the residence but in need of supervision. On the other hand we may have to take into account the possibility that the city and the fortress fell victim to the Kashka people, the ever vigilant enemies of the empire in the north. They could have taken advantage of the transfer of the capital and the resulting weakening of the defense. But although such raids are known to have penetrated at that time almost to the heart of central Anatolia, there is no record of a capture and pillage of Hattusha. Later, however, when Urhi-Teshub (Murshili III) had transferred the residence from Dattashsha back to Hattusha, an incident occurred that has come to our knowledge only quite recently and which seems to fit into this context. In a letter written by the Hittite court to Ramesses II of Egypt we read: "As you, my brother, know the palace of Hatti, should not I know it too . . . burnt down is the palace. What was preserved Urhi-Teshub gave to the great god." This is an allusion to events that happened when Urhi-Teshub was fighting with his rebellious uncle, who later became King Hattushili III. On that occasion the palace was at least partly destroyed. This event took place around 1275 B.C. The victor in this struggle, being a usurper, was scrupulous about traditions and paid special attention to the heart of the empire and its northern buffer zones. He must have quickly embarked on the reconstruction of the citadel. His son and successor, Tuthaliya IV, completed these building operations which resulted in the citadel as we know it. The only two monuments attributable to a specific king belong to Tuthaliya IV: a stela in a poor state of preservation found in the debris near building C, and the fragment of a monumental royal cartouche of black granite unearthed near the gate structure between the lower and upper courtyards (fig. 24). It is presumably a part of a building inscription set over the gate. If this assumption proves to be correct, this important building can be attributed to Tuthaliya IV. In addition, we have noted that buildings A, E, and K yielded archives, the assembling of which is likewise due to the activities of the same Great King. During his lifetime the buildings in question were fully operative until the royal palace sank into dust and ashes, never to rise again.

Figure 24. Gate inscription of Tuthaliya IV. H. originally 0.50 m, W. 0.80 m

The impressive palace complex of the Great Kings, with its lively activities, its army of servants of high and low rank, the court itself and its head the almost godlike king, with the royal chanceries, the envoys and foreign ambassadors who came and went—all this in the form recovered by the excavations, did not last longer than three-quarters of a century. The last documents to be deposited in the archive came from Shuppiluliuma II, who probably lived through the first decade of the 12th century B.C. This cannot be established with accuracy since there is no synchronism for him with Egypt or Assyria. His father Tuthaliya IV was partly contemporary with Tukulti-Ninurta I of Assyria and with Merenptah of Egypt. He himself concluded treaties with Talmi-Teshub, son of Ini-Teshub, king of Carchemish, who had also been a contemporary of his father Tuthaliya IV. These chronological relationships do not help us to fix an exact date for the fall of Hattusha, but clear signs of disaster have been found everywhere in the royal citadel. Not a single building was spared and the surface of the streets and open squares was found covered with thick layers of charred wood and mudbrick reddened by fire.

We do not even know who the enemy was by whose action the city and royal palace of Hattusha fell. A period of inner weakness must have preceded the catastrophe. There are texts which intimate that under the reign of Shuppiluliuma II the inhabitants of the country became rebellious, as is evident from phrases like: "The inhabitants of Hatti sinned against His Majesty" and "when His Majesty, my Lord, found the inhabitants of Hatti to be in revolt." Unlike the fate of the southern parts of the empire where in Cilicia and along the North Syrian coast and far into the hinterland the so-called Peoples of the Sea decisively contributed to the fall of the Hittite power, in the north it must have been old internal and external enemies, especially the Kashka, who exploited the crisis. This time, however, they came not as raiders but as executioners. The fate of the capital and the royal palace was sealed.

IV

YAZILIKAYA

In the summer of 1834, while on a grand tour of Asia Minor, Charles Texier, archaeologist, architect, and, above all, intrepid traveler, reached the area beyond the River Halys which in ancient times was part of Eastern Galatia. There, near the small village called Boğazköy, he was the first European to set eyes on extensive, obviously very ancient ruins. Texier believed these to be the remains of Pteria, the town which Herodotus (I: 76) mentions as having been conquered by Croesus in his war against Cyrus in the middle of the 6th century B.C. Peasants of the Turkish village also led the French traveler to a place which they called Yazılıkaya, "inscribed rock." There they promised to show him a portrait of the Padishah—the Great Lord or Sultan—to them the highest being on earth. As Moslems they could not believe that the image might represent a being from beyond this world. After a little less than half an hour's walk upwards along the rising slope that borders the enclave of Boğazköy to the east, Texier arrived at a large group of rocks and, to his surprise, had in front of him not one picture—and certainly not that of the Padishah—but a whole series of pictures, an entire gallery of reliefs carved out of the natural rock. Texier was immediately followed by the Englishman Hamilton in 1835, but he was himself the first to bring back to Europe the knowledge of this monument. Set in a thinly populated, vast, and barren landscape, Yazilikaya even today leaves a lasting impression on everyone who sees it.

Very soon after the discovery, scholars began to speculate why and when these rock reliefs had been carved. Texier thought that what was represented was a meeting of the Amazons and the Paphlagonians in two processions. Others looked for an explanation in ancient cults: Sandon and Mylitta (that is, Herakles and Astarte) or Baal and Astarte with their retinues were the favorite suggestions so long as a strong Semitic component was still assumed for this part of Asia Minor in the remote past. Even Eduard Meyer was still influenced by this interpretation. He saw in Yazılıkaya a great festive procession of gods and humans on the occasion of the wedding of the God of Heaven to the Goddess of the Earth. Others believed that the reliefs would have been made in connection with a momentous historical event of the area. For example, Hamilton and Barth suggested that the reliefs depicted the signing of the treaty by which the Medes and the Lydians agreed to make the River Halys the frontier between their two empires. Or the representations were thought to render the wedding of Aryenis to Astyages, the children of the Lydian Alyattes and the Mede Kyaxares, a dynastic marriage arranged to seal the treaty in question. It is understandable that such hypotheses prevailed as long as the ruined site and the nearby rock carvings gave no clue as to when exactly they should be dated and to what ancient people they should be attributed. That the city and the rock reliefs were firmly interrelated was obvious from the beginning and was generally accepted, although there were still some doubts until shortly before the Second

World War. In a searching study published in 1933 the Viennese Orientalist Victor Christian still maintained that the rock reliefs were considerably later than the city.

As we have seen, the ruins of Boğazköy have turned out to be much older than assumed by the discoverer and his immediate successors. The site was identified as the capital of the Hittite Empire through the evidence of the Hittite royal archives. But comprehensive though the Hittite writings are, and invaluable as they also are as a source of information in matters of cult, there is not a single text among the many thousands of cuneiform tablets which directly refers to the rock reliefs of Yazılıkaya and so could provide clues to the name and especially the meaning of the rock formation with its many images. So, we are forced to rely on other methods of inquiry, particularly archaeological observations.

The problem is far from settled, current views vary widely, and the bibliography about Yazılıkaya has become extensive and complicated. This is not surprising. The reliefs make such an immediate impression upon a thoughtful observer, they offer so many problems of interpretation, and in more than one respect they are so mysterious that their fascination is never impaired and their challenge to scholars ever new. Since the days of Texier a large number of Hittite rock carvings have been discovered in an area which is defined in the west by the hinterland of Smyrna (Izmir), in the east by the upper Euphrates, in the north by the southern spurs of the Pontic mountain ranges, and in the south by the Mediterranean coast. These are, however, far inferior to those at Yazılıkaya, in size as well as in quality. They are only single figures or at best isolated groups of figures, while in Yazılıkaya we have an entire cycle that stands out as the most eminent monument of its kind in the land of the Hittites.

The expedition which for many years has been engaged in excavations at Boğazköy has, of course, given Yazılıkaya its proper share of attention. Excavations in 1937, 1938, 1939, and again in 1966 considerably increased our knowledge of the original appearance of the rock sanctuary. And there was a corresponding effort to clarify the meaning of the individual reliefs. Basic progress in this direction was the discovery that the main goddess represented in the rock reliefs had a Hurrian name, Hepat. Next, Emmanuel Laroche succeeded in identifying all the essential deities represented in Yazılıkaya with gods of the Hurrian, not the Hittite, pantheon. This striking discovery was achieved by recognizing their correspondence to the Hurrian deities of oath listed in the Hittite state treaties and through much progress in the reading of the so-called Hittite hieroglyphs. To show the extent of our present-day understanding of the rock sanctuary, we now must turn to the monument itself.

The road that connects the Hittite capital with Yazılıkaya so depends on the contour of the land that its course can be conjectured even though no traces of an artificially built and paved highway remain. The route leaves the city near the northern end of the inhabited area, a district which also contains the largest temple of Hattusha, the temple of the Weather God. A gate that has not yet been excavated but is nevertheless clearly visible in its ruins marks the beginning of the road. First it crosses the bed of a brook, then rises steeply, soon more gently on the other side, crossing an area marked by large and small groups of rocks. Excavations carried out in 1952 have shown that in niches, shelters, and crevices of these rocks burials had been laid during the 17th to 13th centuries B.C., inhumations as well as cremations. Thus, at least one of the large cemeteries of the Hittite capital was located in this area. It is perhaps not without significance that the road connecting the city with the rock sanctuary should run through this necropolis and that the burial rocks lie on either side of the road, if not everywhere, at least in one place in remarkable concentration. Further along the road rises steadily and in a straight line towards Yazılıkaya, a group of rocks which externally hardly differs from similar formations in the vicinity (plate 17b). Inside, however, are two natural chambers of different size and, in addition, a number of small caves and niches. All of these, together with a little creek running nearby, may possibly have favored the choice of this place as a rock sanctuary.

In the large chamber a procession of 66 deities is represented, separated into males and females with one exception in either group. They are arranged in such a way that the gods appear on the left (plate 18) and the goddesses on the right of the entering visitor. Both processions are moving in a partly measured, partly more lively pace towards the back wall of the chamber which carries the main representation (plate 20b). Here the upper god and the upper goddess stand facing each other at the head of their processions. Apart from the main group all the reliefs are of the same size. They are represented in a manner familiar to us from Hittite art: the male figures appear in profile, except for the torso and shoulders which are frontal, while all the female figures are shown in strict profile. Only the seven highest deities in the main relief, four gods and three goddesses, have been emphasized by the artist both in size and by their accompanying symbols. They stand either on conical mountains or on animals, such as the panther, lion, or double-headed eagle, which, in turn, may also be standing on mountains. The main god, however, stands on deities of lower rank, namely, on figures characterized by their attire and their emblems as Mountain gods (plate 19a). These wear conical caps and their heads are bent forward deeply under the weight of the main god. A small ivory statuette (plate 19b) shows a similar Mountain God in three-dimensional rendering. This ivory was found on the lowest terrace of the city area and belongs to the 13th century B.C. While the goddesses at Yazılıkaya with their long, mostly vertically pleated skirts, wide belts, and high *poloi* hardly differ from one another individually, the male deities show a greater variation in detail. Most of them wear the typically Hittite knee-length tunic, shoes with upturned toes, and a pointed cap with one or two horns at the front, a headdress characteristic of the gods. Other gods are winged and in one instance there is a hint of strong motion in the wings, in a primitive way. We also see round caps. The weapons vary, too, for some of the gods are armed with scimitars, others carry clubs; still others are totally unarmed.

On the right-hand side of the chamber, almost directly opposite the main group, is a relief of a Hittite Great King nearly 3 meters high, not connected with the two processions of the gods (plate 21a). He wears a large cloak with a long train at the back; in his left hand he carries a staff, the end of which is curved upwards in a spiral like a *lituus*. On his head he wears a close-fitting round cap, and above his raised right hand appears the royal cartouche of Hittite hieroglyphs crowned by the winged sun disc. The name of the Great King is Tuthaliya, but this does not in itself identify him, since we know at least four kings of that name in Hittite history, two of them in the 14th and 13th centuries: Tuthaliya III before around 1370 B.C. and Tuthaliya IV between 1250 and 1220 B.C.

Some of the figures depicted in these great processions can now be identified with certainty. The great goddess standing on a panther is the goddess Hepat, as noted above and as we learn from the syllabic inscription in hieroglyphs. Opposite her is her consort, the great Weather God of Hatti, identified by the ideographic sign for the Hurrian Teshub. The small god behind the main goddess, carrying an axe on his shoulder and standing on a panther is, according to the accompanying inscription, Sharruma, son of Teshub and Hepat. The figure behind Teshub, standing on mountains, is the Weather God of the city of Hattusha, the Hittite capital. In the series of the smaller deities, the winged figure with a pointed cap, followed by two female deities wearing long skirts, is the Hurrian Shaushga, that is, Ishtar as a goddess of war. As such she appears in the procession of male deities, followed by her attendants Ninatta and Kulitta. Next come the Moon and Sun gods (plate 21b), in a sequence exactly characteristic of the Hurrian pantheon. The Moon God is characterized by the crescent on his cap, the Sun God by the winged sun disc on his head. Still further to the rear, four deities behind the Sun God, is a representation that differs in two respects from all the other reliefs in this chamber (plate 22). First it is rendered frontally, and second the figures are hybrid creatures with human bodies but heads and legs of bulls.

They support a boat or crescent-shaped object with their raised arms and stand on a rectangular pedestal from either side of which two ledges protrude; the pedestal is sunken below the base line of the procession. We have come to know the meaning of this group only recently. What the bull-men carry is the hieroglyphic sign for sky, and the object on which they are standing is the sign for earth, here appropriately sunken below the base line, and thus extending into the underworld. This, then, is a representation of the powers that link the nether world with the upper world, the world in which mankind must live.

It must have become evident by now that the great procession of the gods at Yazılıkaya consists of single figures and single motifs which become parts of the total design only inasmuch as they appear in the rock relief in a meaningful sequence subject to a strict hierarchy. The artist neither attempted nor would he probably have been able to connect the single figures by an inner relationship and through artistic devices current only in later times. But even with its simple sequence and the simple hierarchy, as expressed in the gradation of sizes culminating in the main scene, this gallery offers a most impressive view, impressive especially perhaps because the outcome has been achieved by such simple means.

The separation at Yazılıkaya of the male and female processions corresponds, as Emmanuel Laroche has shown, to the order followed by the Hurrians, not the Hittites, in lists of supranatural powers. But to have arranged the two groups on the two sides of the chamber in such a way that they advance towards each other and so that the two main deities at the head of their pageants confront and meet each other is an independent and original creation of the artist. Was he a Hittite sculptor or was he summoned to the court of Hattusha from the Hurrian world? We do not know. Yet how considerable his accomplishment is and how far it surpasses all the other known contemporary sculptural designs from Anatolia is seen in the arrangement of the two processions so that the leading figures belong to one and the same family of gods. For in the Hurrian pantheon Teshub, the main god, is the consort of Hepat, the main goddess, and Sharruma is their son, who here marches immediately behind his mother. This triad, then, in the central relief of Yazılıkaya links the two processions in a truly significant way.

The sculptor evidently tried to convey this unity also to those who might not be able to understand the hieroglyphic names—Teshub, Hepat, and Sharruma—but had to rely for their understanding on the pictorial representation. In front of the forward leg of Teshub, the front part of a bull is visible. One can also discern the lower contour of its body finely drawn between the legs of the god. Its raised tail is visible behind the sword of the god. Its front legs raised, the animal jumps along beside the god, in the relief partly hidden behind him. This gives the picture a depth which is unusual in Hittite art. The front part of another bull, identical in all essentials, appears before—or rather next to—the main goddess, Hepat, directly opposite its counterpart. Here, however, the outline of the body and the tail are covered by the long pleated skirt of the goddess. Both bulls wear high peaked caps which mark them as divine beings. Now Hepat, the "goddess of heaven," has no relation to divine bulls, but Teshub has. Sheri and Hurri ("day" and "night" in Hurrian) are his companions and through him also those of the Hittite Weather God. They are divine bulls who draw the chariot of the Weather God. In the rock relief of Imamkulu in central Cappadocia, the chariot of the god is represented, the whole team driving over deified mountains. This is a combination similar to that in Yazılıkaya: Weather God, sacred bulls, and mountain gods, except that the chariot does not appear in the rock sanctuary. But there the artist has separated the two bulls, leaving only one with the Weather God Teshub and attributing the other to Hepat, although she has no connection with bulls in her cult. He has, therefore, taken a liberty which is contrary to the known canon of Hittite iconography. The reason for this cannot be that the artist was unable to represent the two bulls standing side by side, overlapping, next to the god Teshub to whom they belong. This would not have worried him, since in the rock relief of Imamkulu cited above the chariot appears as though drawn by only one bull, while in fact there are two. A Hittite sculptor of this time could simply expect an observer to imagine a second bull completely hidden by the first. This would have been true also for Yazılıkaya. The reason the artist put one of the bulls next to Teshub and the other bull beside Hepat, although he was not hers, can only be that he was aiming at symmetry. I believe that he intended to express the close association of the divine couple by confronting not only god with goddess but also Sheri with Hurri, the divine bulls.

This interpretation presupposes,of course, that the identification of the two bull gods with Sheri and Hurri is valid. There would hardly be any reason for dwelling on this had not Emmanuel Laroche recently expressed doubt. The bull standing next to Teshub has an accompanying hieroglyphic inscription consisting of eight, mostly very worn, signs. The uppermost is the ideogram for "god," and the second a sign in which Laroche sees the ideogram for the god Sharruma. He therefore reads the text thus: "Sharruma, bull-calf of Teshub." According to Laroche this god would appear three times in the main composition of Yazılıkaya: (1) connected with Teshub (left bull), (2) as the son of Hepat (right bull), and (3) as the son of the divine couple (the god in human form standing on a panther behind Hepat). If this were correct, we would have an even stronger unity within the main relief at Yazılıkaya. The artist would then have linked the main figures admirably by means of images. But this interpretation cannot be accepted for two reasons. The crucial sign in the inscription of the sacred bull next to Teshub bears a remote resemblance to the ideogram for Sharruma; but it is, in fact, a different sign, namely the sign "bull's head." On closer inspection, the bull beside Hepat also proves to have a hieroglyphic inscription, of which only the uppermost signs remain dimly visible. These certainly differed from those in the counterpart. The ideogram for Sharruma here again is lacking, and with it support for Laroche's interpretation. The inscriptions, therefore, in spite of their deplorable state of preservation, do not contradict the interpretation of the bulls as Sheri and Hurri. This still remains the most probable solution, especially in view of the related rock monument of Imamkulu.

But let us now return to our main subject and examine the rock reliefs as a whole: We saw them previously as a series of individual figures and individual motifs combined into a unified procession of male and female deities. This is without precedent in Hittite art before Yazılıkaya, as far as one can judge from the remaining monuments. But one wonders whether the precursors of Yazılıkaya should be looked for exclusively in monumental art, or perhaps also in the minor arts. It is certain that individual deities, especially the leading gods, were represented as early as the 18th century B.C. This is shown by small lead figurines of gods with high caps, tunics, and scimitars, which correspond precisely to a series of identical gods in Yazılıkaya. Polychrome relief vases, on the other hand, show that as early as the 16th century B.C. individual motifs were juxtaposed to form comprehensive representations of a particular subject. One example was found in Bitik to the northwest of Ankara some twenty years ago, and another, nearly intact, appeared in 1966 at Inandık not far from Çankırı, the ancient Gangra. But in spite of such beginnings, noted, as yet, only in an unfortunately small number of finds, Yazılıkaya is no doubt the first great monumental realization of such an artistic conception.

But what was the meaning of this great procession of gods? What happened in the chamber whose walls bear these reliefs? In other words, apart from the identification of the individual gods and goddesses and besides the fact that we are dealing with deities of the Hurrian pantheon, what was the significance of the whole complex?

Before we turn to this question, we should first examine the small chamber. It is reached through a narrow crevice, artificially widened in ancient times. Its entry is guarded by two lion-headed, winged demons, their paws raised in a protective gesture (plate 23). At the end of this passage, one arrives in a long and rather narrow chamber with walls rising perpendicularly on both sides (plate 24a). They look as if they have been artificially smoothed, but in fact their appearance is the result of old, natural splitting. On entering this chamber, one sees on the right a frieze of twelve identical gods (plate 24b). They correspond to those who bring up the rear of the procession of male deities in the main chamber, with the difference that here they carry sickle-shaped swords. On the opposite side we notice the comparatively well-preserved relief of two figures, 1.70 meters high, the larger characterized by his attributes as a deity, the smaller by his as a Great King (plate 25a). They are represented as moving forward side by side, not independently but linked together in a close relationship which the artist has conveyed in a simple yet most impressive manner. The god extends his left arm around the shoulder of the king and also clasps his right wrist. This gesture expresses that the god will protect as well as guide the king on his path. The inscription, again in hieroglyphs, identifies the god as Sharruma, the same deity who appears in the main chamber standing on a panther behind the Great Goddess. In this case, also, the name of the king is Tuthaliya. His connection with Sharruma as his tutelary god leaves no doubt that here we have the fourth king of that name. This means that this relief can be dated to a particular period, namely to the decades after the middle of the 13th century B.C.

On the same wall, to the left of the king's relief, there is a curious representation (plate 25b). This has given rise to many diverse theories but can now, as we shall see, be explained. One sees a human head, evidently that of a god, as the peaked cap indicates. Directly underneath there are two lion protomes whose heads and raised paws face left and right respectively. Below these are two antithetical lions hanging head down and finally, attached to the lower lions, there is a double-edged blade with a distinct midrib. Below this the rock shows traces of cuttings for the limestone paving slabs which once covered the floor of this chamber. There can be no doubt that this relief is meant to represent a sword fixed in the ground. It shows the upper part of the blade, the hilt formed by the figures of the lions, and the pommel in the shape of the head of a god. The sword evidently belongs to the divine realm; perhaps it is the emblem of a specific god.

On the same rock-face, to the left of the Sword God, there is a roughly worked, unfinished figure. It is impossible to tell what the representation would have been, but these traces may indicate that more work was envisaged at Yazılıkaya and left undone when the city and the rock sanctuary perished.

Further to the left there follows the name of a Hittite Great King with the familiar winged sun disc crowning the group of signs. This cartouche is separate and not connected with any representation. Here, too, the hieroglyphs indicate the name of a King Tuthaliya, but without any clue to his specific identification. The same cartouche is known to us from the impression of a royal seal on a bulla.

It is readily apparent that the reliefs in this small chamber differ from those in the great gallery. They are single motifs throughout which are neither arranged in a meaningful order, nor connected in an obvious manner. In one respect, however, they are unified. With the exception of the isolated cartouche, all the figures in the reliefs either move to the north (the twelve gods on the west side) or face north (the gods and the Great King, and, logically, also the hieroglyphs in figural form). It has therefore plausibly been concluded that all these reliefs had once been related to a monument in the north of this chamber, possibly a figure in the round, a statue perhaps of an ancestor, a namesake of the Tuthaliya who appears with his tutelary god Sharruma (plate 25a).

We want to return briefly to this relief since it illustrates what has been said before about the transfer of minor art motifs into monumental art. The same way of showing the Hittite Great King and his tutelary god is known from glyptic art, namely, on seals of Great Kings. We have an excellent example from Boğazköy in the impression of a seal of King Muwatalli, about 1300 B.C. (plate 25c). Another no less impressive example occurs on a cuneiform tablet from Ras Shamra, ancient Ugarit, in North

Syria. In the center of the tablet is the impression of a seal of the Great King Tuthaliya IV, guided and protected by his personal god; the god and the king here appear in the same attire. The motif has, indeed, been known to us indirectly for a long time. In the Egyptian version of the treaty concluded by Ramesses II in his twenty-first year (*c.* 1270 B.C.) with King Hattushili III (recorded at Karnak and at the Ramesseum), the seal of the treaty is described as follows:

> What is in the middle of the tablet of silver. On the front side: a figure consisting of the image of Seth, embracing an image of the Great Prince of Hatti, surrounded by a border inscribed with these words: "The seal of Seth, the ruler of Heaven, the seal of the treaty, which Hattushili made, the great Prince of Hatti, the mighty, the son of Murshili, the Great Prince of Hatti, the mighty."

The silver tablet is not preserved, but the seal surely resembled the impressions from Boğazköy (plate 25c) and Ras Shamra as much as the relief in the small chamber at Yazılıkaya. This relief used to be attributed to Hattushili III, wrongly but understandably, before the Hittite evidence became known. We now know that this motif of the tutelary god embracing and guiding the Great King was typical of the great state seals, at least from about 1300 B.C. and that the same representation, as Yazılıkaya proves, was adopted in monumental art.

We can recapitulate now as follows. The reliefs in the two chambers do not differ in style or form; it is clear that they belong to the same artistic convention. However, the representations appear on the walls in a different arrangement. In the larger chamber, we have processions of male and of female deities which meet in the main scene where the respective supreme deities are brought face to face. In the small chamber we find reliefs which are complete in themselves, isolated without any visible interconnection. Beside the gods there are two figures of Hittite Great Kings. They are not portrayed in an individual manner but are stereotypes. Both their names are, according to the hieroglyphic inscriptions accompanying them, Tuthaliya, who, as we have seen, occurs several times in the Hittite king list but among a great many other royal names. The unique position of this particular name at Yazılıkaya is emphasized by the isolated cartouche in the small chamber which also contains the name of Tuthaliya. It is, therefore, not surprising that many scholars —particularly Emmanuel Laroche—concluded that Yazılıkaya as a whole was created at the time of Tuthaliya IV, shortly after 1250 B.C. The monument would thus have existed only during the last decades of the Hittite Empire until the catastrophe around 1200 B.C.

This rock sanctuary, as many have said, may well have been regarded as a place of manifestation of the divine powers long before it was provided with reliefs. But excavations in front of the complex conducted shortly before the last war and in 1966 have shown that this place of worship was more than just an open-air sanctuary (figs. 25, 26). The group of rocks and rock-chambers was connected with architectural constructions which, while they did not change the rock-complex fundamentally, made it part of an extensive cult-precinct. Approaching the sanctuary via the Hittite processional road, one first entered a large, isolated propylon with a staircase leading to a higher terrace. Then, through a smaller gate, one reached a rectangular courtyard flanked on two sides by small rooms of varying sizes. At its far end were the foundations of an altar and a small single-room structure which was probably used for lustrations. Turning at a right angle to the left, one arrived through another gateway in the forecourt which gave access to the main chamber with the great procession of the gods and also to the smaller chamber through the special rock passage. This rather elaborate architectural complex (whose predecessor, a long irregular wall, merely closed the rock-chamber on the outside) is basically similar to other examples of contemporary Hittite sacral architecture with its propylon, court, and house for lustrations, and with the approximately axial alignment of these parts. The large temple buildings of the nearby capital are typical. The standard Hittite temple

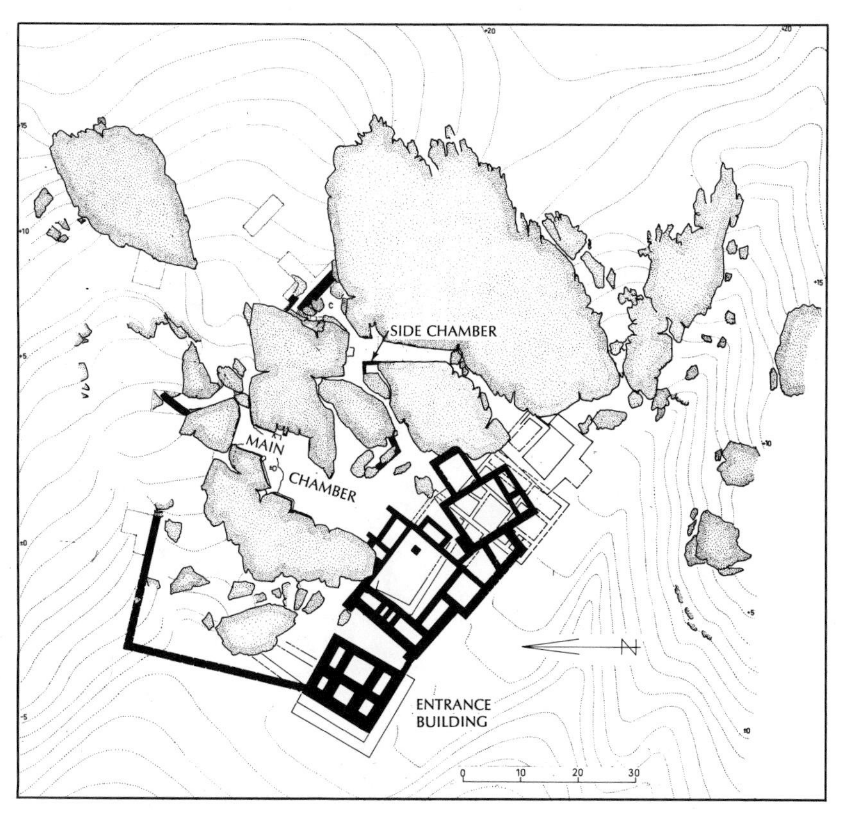

Figure 25. Yazılıkaya: general plan of complex

has the adyton or holy of holies at the rear of the court, shifted slightly to the left or right of the main axis. But in Yazılıkaya, the adyton (the rock-chamber with the great procession) lies at a right angle to the other parts of the building. This deviation was obviously determined by the lie of the land at Yazılıkaya which did not allow the usual alignment from propylon to adyton.

The constructions in front of the rock-chambers which transformed the complex into a temple proper underwent radical alterations during their existence, at least in the back section behind the court. The rooms there, destroyed by a fire of un-

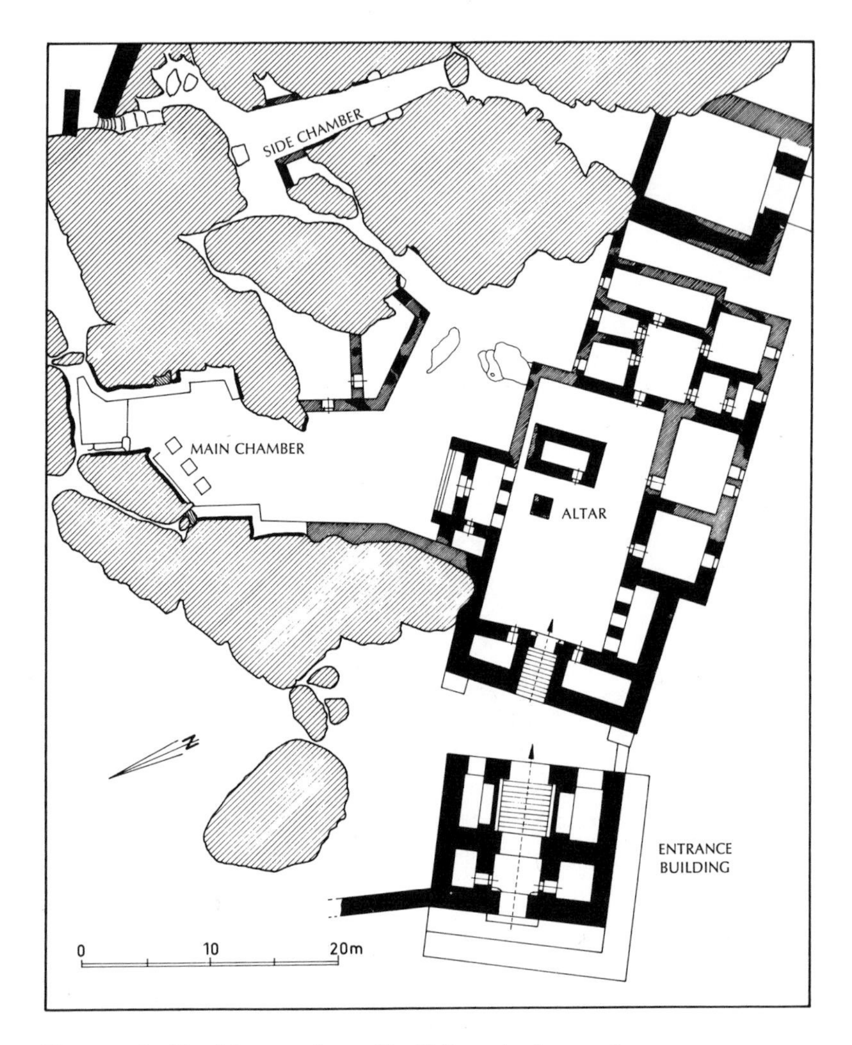

Figure 26. Yazılıkaya: plan of buildings in front of sanctuary

known origin, were rebuilt with a quite different orientation; the depth of the court was reduced and the number of rooms greatly diminished. One has the impression that this new construction was deliberately oriented towards the rock entrance of the small chamber.

Thus, Yazılıkaya, with all its architectural elaboration, at least in plan had begun to resemble the normal Hittite temple, although it is certain that the rock-chambers were never covered but remained open to the sky. But recent soundings near the foundations show that the similarities have definite limits. Hittite temples, wherever we know them—in Boğazköy, Hüyük near Alaca, or in Cilician Tarsus—are distinguished by very solid construction, especially by foundations which are most carefully put together. At Yazılıkaya, however, the buildings, except for the propylon, were erected in a strikingly careless manner. The foundations hardly anywhere go down to bedrock but are usually set on rubble. The stones, even for the visible socles of the walls, were selected casually. Sometimes stones were reused from other buildings and the joints of the individual blocks often do not fit properly. It is, therefore, quite evident that here, unlike the city temples some of which at least were several storeys high, we are dealing with buildings of one storey only. The lightly constructed buildings in front of Yazılıkaya could hardly have withstood the regular ritual usage attested for the daily cult in a normal Hittite temple. One can well imagine that the type of construction was determined by the purpose of the complex and that the sanctuary was used only on special limited occasions in the course of the year.

This interpretation, based on the character of the construction, would not have been offered with such confidence if it did not point in the same direction as other indications concerning the meaning of the great procession of the gods in the main chamber. As long ago as 1918, Zimmern suggested—briefly and without documentation—that Yazılıkaya might have been a House of the New Year's Festival, like the *bit akitu* of the Babylonians. Walter Andrae and Benno Landsberger adopted his view without being able to add supporting evidence. But now we have a text, recently published by Heinrich Otten, which at least reveals that the Hittites also celebrated a special kind of festival at the beginning of the New Year. It reads:

> In honor of the Weather God at (?) the beginning of the New Year a great festival of heaven and earth was celebrated. All the gods assembled and entered into the house of the Weather God. Whichever god harbors anger (?) in his soul shall chase the evil anger (?) from his soul. (Now) eat at this feast, drink! Satisfy your hunger and quench your thirst. The King's and the Queen's life hail! (Hea)ven's and the earth's (life)(?) hail! the grain's life (hail!)

We also know, especially from the ritual of the AN-TAHSHUM plant, that of the two great annual Hittite festivals, the spring and the autumn festivals, the first had a special significance, inasmuch as it was celebrated outside the city in open, unsettled country. Since the Hittite new year also began in the spring, the festival of the new year probably coincided or was indeed identical with the festival of the spring. This does not in itself prove that the festivities and ceremonies were actually performed at Yazılıkaya, but it seems very likely that this sanctuary may be regarded as a House of the New Year's Festival, an institution of Babylonian origin here represented in native Hittite form.

If we favor this interpretation on the strength of the present evidence, it applies only to the temple buildings in front of the main chamber and to the great procession but not equally to the small chamber which, as we have seen, differs so much in its essential features.

In the course of the spring festival, the ritual of the eleventh day prescribes a visit to the mortuary temple. It says:

> The highest palace official ushers the year into the mortuary temple, followed by the king.

What is called "year'" in this passage must be a symbol embodying the concept.

The excavations at Yazılıkaya in 1966 have shown that the rock-sanctuary also served a sepulchral purpose. In two deep crevices along the northern outer edge we found burials which, although much disturbed in later times, can be dated on ceramic evidence to the period of the Hittite Empire. In addition, in the same crevices, curious pavements came to light in a series of superposed levels which suggest that a succession of sacrifices had taken place. Burials, likewise disturbed but nevertheless still clearly discernible, were also found in a cavity in the rock between the main chamber and the passage leading to the small chamber. And here, along with the remains of human skeletons, bird skeletons came to light. In one instance, a bird had been pinned down and intentionally confined in a small depression by fourteen bronze nails stuck vertically in the ground. This surely is a bird sacrifice which, as we know, played an important role in the cult of the underworld. For example, in a ritual incantation against the impurity of the house we read:

> Then he sacrifices a lamb (and) eight birds to those of the underworld.

And it is precisely deities of the underworld who are prominent in the reliefs of the small chamber.

We have already noted the curious representation of the so-called Sword God with a hilt in the shape of lions. It was suggested long ago that this motif—if not in its specific form, at least in its basic concept—goes back to the Hurrian artistic tradition of North Syria and North Mesopotamia. This assumption is corroborated by a bronze sword found not long ago in the region of Diyarbakır. The hilt, as in the Yazılıkaya representation, is decorated with two antithetical lions suspended heads down. A cuneiform inscription dates the object to the Old Assyrian period and states that the sword was brought as a votive offering (which accounts for the rather flimsy manufacture of the weapon) into a temple of the god Nergal, the god of the underworld. This sword, made as a ritual offering to Nergal, sufficiently resembles the Sword God in Yazılıkaya to make us wonder whether the sword relief is also somehow connected with a deity of the underworld. A text published by Heinrich Otten strongly supports this idea. This ritual text mentions eight gods of the past, most of them with Hurrian names, who had been banished to the underworld by the ruling Weather God. By invocations and offerings, the incantation priests can reach these magic powers. The ritual says of the incantation priest:

> He makes these gods out of clay. He makes them as swords and fixes them into the ground.

Whom would this not remind of the sword in the small chamber of Yazılıkaya, stuck into the ground and divine, because surmounted by the head of a god? Moreover, Güterbock has recently published a ritual in which the "Bronze swords of Nergal, of the 'blood-stained Nergal,' and the twelve gods of the cross-roads" are mentioned side by side. Twelve gods as a unit occur only once in the texts and that is here in connection with Nergal. But twelve gods in a tight group appear on the wall of the right side of the small chamber just opposite the Sword God. So strong are the allusions to the deities of the underworld, or, indeed, to the god of the underworld himself, that the original purpose of this section of Yazılıkaya surely must be connected with the underworld. One cannot avoid the impression that this chamber was a temple of the dead, say the funeral temple for a king named Tuthaliya.

It may even seem that we have a direct reference to this funerary temple in a tablet found recently in Boğazköy. In it, Shuppiluliuma II, the last Hittite king known to us, during or shortly after whose reign the capital perished (*c.* 1200 B.C.), says that he had a statue of his father Tuthaliya made and a *hegur* built; subsequently he had the sculpture brought into the *hegur* and erected there. *Hegur* means "summit of the rock," "peak," a term referring to man-made, artificial structures, which Otten interprets as a permanent rock sanctuary. As such it could indeed be the small chamber at Yazılıkaya. However, in the upper city of the capital itself there is a rock, today called Nişantepe, which has on its east side a large, unfortunately much-weathered hieroglyphic inscription of Shuppiluliuma II, the Great King just mentioned (plate 14a). In this text, the deeds of his father Tuthaliya seem to be narrated at great length. This rock also once had an extensive man-made superstructure as proved by beddings and cuttings in the rock surface. Nişantepe, then, was obviously also a *hegur*. Because of the inscription of Shuppiluliuma II, it has a more than equal claim to be the monument mentioned in the text about this king's *hegur*.

Regrettable as it may be that no certain literary testimony regarding the small chamber of Yazılıkaya can be gained from this or other texts, this does not detract from the otherwise plausible interpretation of this chamber as a temple of the dead. The adyton of this shrine seems to have been in the northeast of the rock-chamber. There a deep niche, investigated during the excavations of 1966, is closed off at the back by a heavy wall consisting of mighty limestone boulders. But at the exact point where the rock chamber merges into this niche, the isolated hieroglyphic cartouche of a Great King Tuthaliya is carved on the rock. It seems thus that this cartouche had a special relevance to the niche. To this particular spot future excavations will have to pay special attention.

After the fall of the Hittite capital, Yazılıkaya did not perish altogether. The architectural structures tumbled down and vanished, because they lost their meaning when the Hittite cult ceased. But the ancient images of the gods survived. None of them fell a victim to intentional destruction, although internally and externally political and ethnic conditions changed completely after the fall of the Hittite Empire and traditions were interrupted to a great extent. Phrygian finds, however, such as a vase of the 6th century B.C., burials of around 500 B.C., and some objects belonging to the time when these regions were part of Hellenistic and Roman Galatia, prove that the rock-chambers were still visited and even used. Obviously, these figures carved on the rock and intended by their creators to remain forever did not lose their vigor, although to later generations in a changed world they spoke in a different language and were given names unknown to us. And do not they speak to us today when we approach them with open minds? After such a visit, who could forget the quiet site and its grand, rugged setting, or fail to remember the haunting presence of the ancient gods?

V

THE HITTITE EMPIRE AND EGYPT IN THE LIGHT OF THE EXCAVATIONS AND ARCHIVES OF BOĞAZKÖY

In September 1931 at the start of the second series of campaigns at Boğazköy, a tall, slender vase of alabaster was found in the citadel of the Hittite Great Kings. The vase is damaged at the rim and chipped slightly, but otherwise intact. Its material and shape indicate distinctly that it is not of local manufacture. It was imported to Anatolia either from Syrian territory which during the 18th Dynasty and earlier part of the 19th Dynasty was strongly influenced by Egyptian culture, or from Egypt itself.

This find did not come as a surprise, since it was known that relations existed between the Hittites and Egypt in the 14th and 13th centuries B.C. Our knowledge came from the Egyptian record of the treaty concluded between Ramesses II and Hattushili III, some letters among the Tell el Amarna documents, two of which are from the Hittite Great King Shuppiluliuma, and some cuneiform tablets found by Hugo Winckler in Boğazköy in 1906 and 1907. Moreover, the alabaster vase at the time of its discovery was not the only known Egyptian import in Anatolia. As early as 1882 a statuette of black granite had been found in Adana. This represents a kneeling woman, a nurse by the name of Sitsneferu, dating from the Middle Kingdom, most likely from the time of Sesostris II (1897-1879 B.C.). Admittedly, the object when found was not *in situ* but had been built into a later wall. However, this is no reason for suggesting that it had been carried off from Egypt in recent or even modern times.

We may, rather, assume that the statuette reached Cilicia from Syria during the Middle Kingdom when the Egyptians had gained a foothold in Gubla (Byblos) and, to a lesser degree, in Ugarit (Ras Shamra) on the northern coast. Also of Middle Kingdom date is a statuette of black basalt, which is a portrait of a man named Keri, as the inscription indicates. This sculpture was discovered in Kırıkkale, 35 miles east of Ankara, in 1926. There is a large mound in Kırıkkale, partly of natural rock, partly artificial, the site of a city and a citadel with strong fortifications and miscellaneous finds dating back to the third millennium B.C. This Egyptian statuette must have been originally imported to the ancient town, although it was found reused in a late tomb. Unfortunately, the site has never been more closely investigated, since it is entirely covered with and surrounded by modern industrial buildings. Unlike Adana which faces Syria beyond the Taurus, Kırıkkale lies north of the Taurus Mountains in the heart of Anatolia, in the core of the Old Hittite lands about 62 miles from Hattusha as the crow flies. In addition, there is a Bes figure of bone from Alaca Hüyük, located 15 miles north-northeast of Boğazköy. The style and details of this Bes figure assign it also to the time of the Middle Kingdom. According to the excavators it was "found in the deepest layer of the Hittite period." There is a second relevant find from Alaca Hüyük, a bone plaque incised with a representation of the Osiris symbol, the so-called djed-pillar. The ceramic context dates this to the 18th century B.C., thus providing an *ante quem* date for its manufacture. The associated pottery corresponds to that from level Ib of kārum Kanesh at Kültepe and from level 4 of the northern lower city of Boğazköy.

It is very likely that these objects of Egyptian or Syrian origin dating from the time of the Middle Kingdom reached Central Anatolia by way of Syrian towns of a certain cultural importance. The Bes figure and the djed-pillar must have been transferred shortly after they had been made, as is evident from their stratigraphic context in Anatolia. The statuette of Keri from Kırıkkale, on the other hand, which was not found in its original context, may have come to Central Anatolia as late as the later 15th or even the 14th century when Hittite kings were active in Syria. It might have been a present or a piece of booty from a Syrian town or a Syrian royal palace where it could have been kept for a long time. However that may be, these scattered finds and the alabaster vase from Boğazköy proper led one to expect that the excavations at Boğazköy-Büyükkale would yield further Egyptian imports illustrating the direct or indirect relations between Egypt and Hatti. Today, now that Büyükkale has been fully excavated, one has to admit that these hopes have not been fulfilled. Here and in the other parts of the city which have, thus far, been investigated, only two Egyptian objects of note have come to light, apart from some scarabs which do not yield safe historical evidence. One is a small fragment of a stela of red Assuan granite with remnants of a hieroglyphic inscription (fig. 27). What is preserved of the text is difficult to interpret. W. Stevenson Smith recently proposed the following reading: "beloved of the Ennead of Heliopolis in Kheri-aha," which is an ancient sanctuary on the east bank of the Nile, south of Old Cairo and east of Memphis. The stela belongs to the earlier 19th Dynasty. It was found in that part of the palace complex which we regard as the audience hall, although we do not know its precise original location in the building.

The other find does not come from the palace but was excavated in 1960 in the so-called House on the Slope south of the Great Temple (Temple I). It is particularly unfortunate that this piece was not found in a good context but in mixed debris. The

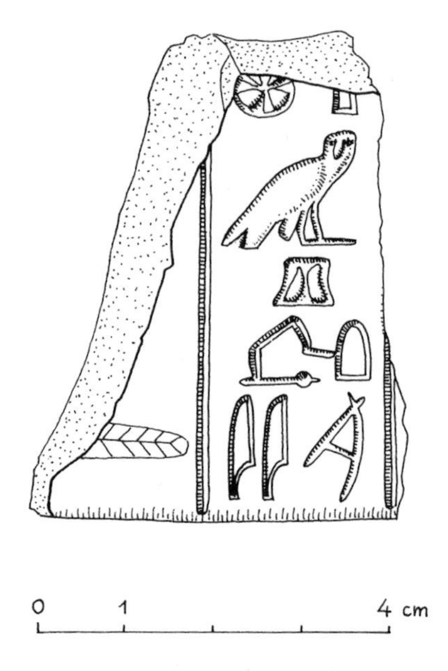

Figure 27. Fragment of Egyptian stela in red granite, 19th Dynasty. H. 0.057 m, W. 0.04 m

object is a fragment of a vase made of obsidian (volcanic glass) and bears the name of the famous Hyksos king Khyan (fig. 28). The quality and the elegance of the hieroglyphic signs are proof that the vase is a product of Egypt and that it was inscribed there with the royal cartouche. Khyan was one of the most important of the six Hyksos rulers of the 15th Dynasty. The origin and the ethnic affinity of these foreign conquerors who gained control over Egypt are still a mystery to us and a much discussed problem. Indeed, Khyan cannot yet be identified with any of the names recorded by Manetho for Hyksos rulers. It is certain, however, that he is to be placed before Apophis, the fourth of Manetho's Hyksos. Under Apophis, the Theban district was lost to the Hyksos but Khyan still ruled over and built in Gebelen, considerably to the south of Thebes. He must thus be earlier than Apophis and before the beginning of the 16th century B.C.

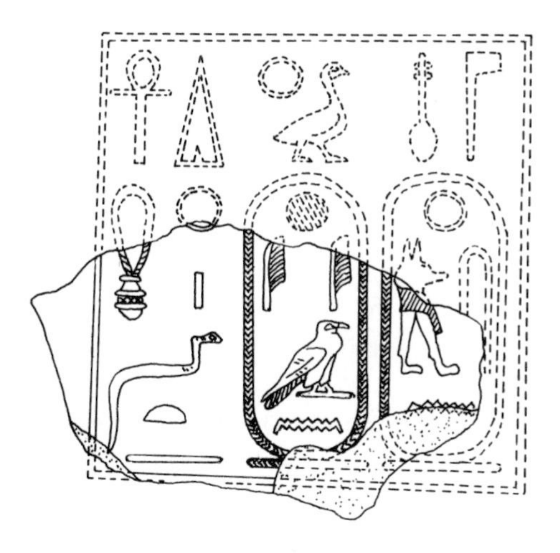

Figure 28. Inscription on Khyan vase restored. H. 0.029 m, W. 0.059 m

Khyan is the only Hyksos ruler for whom we have evidence, other than scarabs, outside of Egypt. His name appears on a small calcite jar-lid found by Evans in the foundations of the second palace of Knossos in Crete and also on a basalt lion which appeared in the antiquities market of Baghdad. Whether this lion reached the East in ancient or more recent times must be left undecided. However, the ointment-jar lid from Knossos and the obsidian vase from Hattusha, which one might also interpret as a perfume container, are authentic finds of the Hyksos period from places outside the Egyptian realm. We cannot simply declare both of them as "verschleppt," displaced, as has been done recently by W. Helck. We would give much to know exactly how such a precious object signed with the name of a pharaoh of the 15th Dynasty came to Hattusha. One would not like to think of commercial relations, since royal possessions were normally not commercially traded. The vase may well have arrived at the court of a foreign dynasty as a present, but hardly straight to Hattusha which at that time had no direct relations with the court of the pharaohs. The Syrian residence of a dynast of Hurrian descent is a more likely place of origin for the vase. How it reached the Hittite capital we can but conjecture. It seems possible that the obsidian container, after having been kept as an heirloom at a Syrian court for a long time, was brought either as a present or as booty to Hattusha. In Egypt itself the names of the Hyksos kings were thoroughly erased from the monuments after the fall of their dynasty. At a Syrian court, however, this need not necessarily have happened. It is, nevertheless, possible that the vase of Khyan found its way from Syria to Boğazköy much earlier, at about the time of the Hittite kings Hattushili I or Murshili I. Both were active in Syria and captured important cities in that country; the former dealt with Alalah (Tell Atchana) and the latter with Halpa (Aleppo). To what extent booty was carried off to Hattusha on such an occasion we learn from the annals of Hattushili I. Since he and his successor Murshili are separated from Khyan by fifty years at most, the vase would not have stayed long in Syria. Besides, this interpretation would spare us the predicament of having to explain how the precious vessel bearing the name of an outlawed ruler could have survived the overthrow of the Hyksos, even in Syria.

To summarize, we can say that the number of objects of Egyptian origin found in Hittite territory of Asia Minor, especially in the capital of the empire, is extremely small. This fact, reflecting the present state of research, in no way mirrors the actual situation in antiquity. This is evident from the texts which mention a wealth of objects now lost, purloined, or destroyed and—in any case—no longer preserved. Import and export were reciprocal. To give only a few examples, vessels of gold went from Egypt to the Hittite court, while silver vessels traveled in the opposite direction. Clothes were exchanged, furniture was sent from Egypt to Hatti. Yet we are not told in detail what these imports looked like. The only descriptions we have are like the following which comes from a letter of Shuppiluliuma about vessels which he is sending to the court of the pharaoh: "One *bibru* offering vessel of silver in the shape of a stag, five minas in weight, another of silver in the shape of a ram, three minas in weight." In another letter "one box, the front of which is inlaid in the Egyptian manner with gold and lapislazuli" is mentioned as having been delivered to Hattusha. Such laconic descriptions cannot replace the originals, which alone would enable us to understand fully the exchange of goods and to evaluate to what extent the imports may have influenced the arts and crafts in each country.

We are compensated for this incomplete state of the material finds, however, by other evidence. The remarkable increase of texts from the archives has widened and deepened our knowledge of the political as well as the personal relations between the Hittite and the Egyptian courts. Our knowledge of one particular period, namely that of the reign of Hattushili III and Ramesses II is now more profound and detailed than one could have expected. But before we turn our attention to this aspect of the finds from Hattusha, a brief survey of the historical background is called for.

During the Middle Kingdom, particularly during the 12th Dynasty (1991-1792 B.C.) Egypt had expanded its interests far into western Asia up to the Lebanon which supplied her with the necessary timber. Above all others, the coastal town of Byblos was closely related to Egypt and was almost Egyptian in character. The local king was looked upon as a special kind of Egyptian official. His appointment was sanctioned by the dispatch of a precious ointment-vessel by the Egyptian court. Farther north, in Ugarit, the monuments of Amenemhat III and Sesostris II also attest to a strong Egyptian influence which is much less evident in the interior, for instance, in Qatna. Lacking other sources, we cannot determine whether the erection of royal monuments (especially sphinxes which are, of course, symbols of Egyptian rulers) expressed a claim of Egyptian sovereignty. In any case the Mari letters of the 18th century B.C., in which we find references to a number of places in the interior of Syria, Qatna among them, do not mention Egypt. Nevertheless, judging from the remaining monuments, the trade on the coast and along the coastal areas must have been very lively. The Egyptian bases at Byblos, and possibly also at Ugarit, were above all concerned with this trade and its protection. But all this was lost, especially when the Hyksos, literally "rulers of the foreign countries," seized power in Egypt. One of them was Khyan, whom we know from the obsidian vase in Boğazköy.

Reaction against the foreign rule set in towards the middle of the 16th century, initiating in Upper Egypt. The kings of the 18th Dynasty gained supremacy over Palestine and Syria mainly due to the campaigns of Tuthmosis III. They made the princes of the small Syrian states loyal to themselves, partly by means of garrisons, partly by means of treaties, retaining them as outposts against the peoples of the more remote parts of western Asia. There the Hittites were just at that moment about to expand their power, pushing forward across the Taurus Mountains to the south. This was not their first appearance in North Syria. Kings Hattushili I and Murshili I, as mentioned above, had carried out military operations there in the 16th century. Their successes did not endure, since Murshili's successor, Hantili, suffered a setback by the Hurrians near Carchemish. The Hittites were then once again confined to the Anatolian territories north of the Taurus. The Mitanni state established itself in Upper Mesopotamia and North Syria. The Hittite Empire went through a period of great inner weakness which lasted almost a hundred years and prevented the Hittites from interfering effectively in Syria. A Hittite king, either Zidanta or Huzziya, sent tribute to Tuthmosis III in 1471 B.C. and again eight years later. This is understandable since the Egyptian king had forced back the troops of Mitanni to the regions east of the Euphrates, and provided relief for hard-pressed Hatti. At the same time an agreement was signed between the two courts to the effect that the inhabitants of the North Anatolian town of Kurushtama, which is to be sought in the region of the River Iris, would be transferred to Egyptian territory. This event, the cause and extent of which are quite obscure to us, occurred within the framework of a treaty which was subsequently referred to time and again.

Shortly after the middle of the 15th century, under the Great King Tuthaliya III, Hatti first renewed its intreference in North Syria, defeated Mitanni, and concluded a treaty with Aleppo. This had been made possible principally because the Egyptians under Amenhotep II had withdrawn from their former sphere of influence in North Syria. Naturally, the reappearance of the Hittites in this area brought Mitanni and Egypt more closely together. Their respective kings, Artatama and Tuthmosis III, established markedly friendly relations between their two countries. The result for Hatti was a new collapse of its position south of the Taurus, at a time when there were also upheavals of vassal states in Anatolia, and hostile invasions in Anatolian territory. But with the accession of the Great King Shuppiluliuma I a personality appeared on the throne of Hatti who brought the internal and external troubles under control, eliminated the Mitanni state, and persistently asserted himself in Syria.

Shuppiluliuma (*c.* 1370-1335 B.C.) exploited the neglect of Egyptian interests in Syria under the aging Amenhotep III and, to an even greater extent, profited from the inactivity of the next Egyptian pharaoh, Amenhotep IV. It is true he corresponded with both pharaohs and even wrote to Amenhotep IV (Akhenaten) on the occasion of his accession to the throne in accordance with the protocol of the times. Nevertheless, relations remained cool and the correspondence with the Egyptian court seems to have ceased after the third letter to Amenhotep. Shuppiluliuma completely eliminated Mitanni as an independent power, carried out two successful wars in Syria, and captured Carchemish on the Euphrates. He reduced Aleppo, further to the west, to vassalage and made these great old cities bulwarks of the Hittite Empire. He also conspired with the princes of Central and South Syria who owed allegiance to Egypt by treaty. This was bound to lead sooner or later to a serious conflict with Egypt. In fact, it is quite obvious from our sources that from then onwards the relations between Hatti and Egypt became increasingly strained, finally resulting in armed clashes even during the reign of Shuppiluliuma himself. We can explore the history, the development, and the scope of these relations by means of the documents found in the excavations in Boğazköy-Hattusha supplemented occasionally by Egyptian sources.

There is, first of all, a text discovered as early as 1906 by Hugo Winckler and much discussed since then. This text has received important and illuminating additions owing to our 1931-33 excavations of archive A on Büyükkale in Boğazköy. Curiously enough, it is concerned with an incident one would not immediately expect in this context. It occurred when Shuppiluliuma was besieging Carchemish and Amenhotep IV and both his successors Semenkhara and Tutankhamen, after brief reigns of four and nine years respectively, had died. While Shuppiluliuma was besieging Carchemish, a messenger brought him a letter from the Egyptian queen. She was the recently widowed wife of Tutankhamen. The text reads:

> My husband has died, and I have no son. But of you it is said that you have many sons. If you would send me one of your sons, he could become my husband and a king for the country of Egypt. I will on no account accept one of my servants and make him my husband.

The incident is so unprecedented that we can only find some explanation in the extraordinary predicament of the dowager queen. With her husband's death, the ruling dynasty, the 18th, had practically become extinct. Pretenders were scheming so that the dowager queen, in order to save the authority and influence of her house, felt compelled to offer her hand in marriage to a foreign prince who would thus ascend the throne of Egypt. In the eyes of the Egyptians this was, indeed, a most unusual step, all the more so as the queen requested a prince from a country hostile towards Egypt at that time. We know how the Hittite king reacted to this request from a document found in Boğazköy in 1937. The passage reads as follows:

> Then he summoned the Great Ones to an assembly and said: "Such a thing has never happened to me in my whole life."

> And then he sent Hattusha-Ziti, the private secretary, to Egypt, in order to find out what truth there was in the matter with the woman.

The king's remark in the council that such a demand was without precedent eloquently expresses the surprise and suspicion aroused in him by this request which was in sharp contrast to the normally exclusive attitude of the Egyptian court. In the following spring he received in Hattusha another letter from the dowager queen through an Egyptian messenger called Hani. She reproached him for his lack of confidence and repeated her request with more urgency. The Egyptian envoy said in the opening sentence of his speech to the Hittite Great King:

> My lord! This is a humiliation to our country. If we had [a prince] would we have gone to another country to demand a Lord for us?

The Hittite king eventually gave in and sent a prince named Zannanza, who lost his life at the Egyptian border since in the meantime another dynasty, the 19th, had seized power in Egypt. It is obvious that following this event the relations between the two countries were bound to deteriorate even further. In revenge, Shuppiluliuma went on a campaign against the Egyptian country of Amqa.

The kings of the 19th Dynasty, first Horemheb and then especially Ramesses II, set out energetically to realign Syria firmly with Egypt and so to set a limit to the Hittite southward expansion. Thus, inevitably, the moment drew nearer when the sovereignty over Syria would have to be settled by force of arms.

The impending actions were prepared for most carefully by both sides, the Hittites being in a favorable position inasmuch as the Great King Muwatalli in his new residence Dattashsha, in the Lower Land, was nearer to the Syrian theater of operations. The actual cause of the war was the defection of the country of Amurru, west of the Orontes. Tuthaliya IV says the following about this event in the treaty concluded some fifty years later with king Shaushga-muwa of Amurru:

> But when Muwatalli, the brother of the father of My Sun, became king, the people of Amurru wronged him and they let him know this: "Loyal servants we have been, but now we are no longer your servants," and they allied themselves with the king of Egypt. Then the brother of the father of My Sun, Muwatalli, and the king of Egypt fought for the servants of the country of Amurru."

The two armies clashed at Qadesh, not far from Homs in Central Syria in the fifth year of the reign of Ramesses II, in 1285 B.C. Thanks to the sequences of reliefs preserved on the walls of several Egyptian temples, above all on the Ramesseum in Thebes, and to literary and even poetic descriptions, it is possible to reconstruct the Egyptian version of the course of this battle fairly fully. We see there groups of war chariots and infantry colliding, and we can recognize the Hittite Great King on his chariot. We also see Ramesses II who depicts himself as having turned the nearly lost battle into an Egyptian victory almost singlehandedly with the aid of his bodyguard, after having been deserted by all his other armies and troops. In Hittite monumental art, which is largely concerned with cult and ritual and hardly ever illustrates secular scenes, this decisive political event was not depicted. However, it is hinted at in some cuneiform texts found in Hattusha-Boğazköy, the proper context of which has only recently been recognized. It was apparently known at the Hittite court that Ramesses II attributed the alleged victory solely to himself and his bodyguard without any direct participation by his armies. In a note exchanged several decades later, the Hittite Great King Hattushili III must have somewhat ironically alluded to this claim. In an extant letter Ramesses answered him thus:

> In answer to what you are saying with regard to my armies asking: "Were there really no armies?" it has to be said: one of my armies was amidst the country of Amurru, another

> one in the country XXX, and yet another one in the country of Taminta, indeed!

Another text found in Boğazköy, however, briefly and in a lapidary style describes how the events were seen from the Hittite point of view, a version corroborated by the immediate results of the battle:

> At the time when king Muwatalli made war against the king of Egypt, when he defeated the king of Egypt, the Egyptian king went back to the country of Aba. But then king Muwatalli defeated the country of Aba, then he marched back to the country of Hatti, but I remained in the country of Aba.

This text dates from the time of king Hattushili, the brother and successor of Muwatalli. So Muwatalli had left Hattushili behind as the administrator of the newly gained country of Aba, the district around and north of Damascus. From this fact as well as from the positions of power immediately following the battle of Qadesh, it is evident that the Egyptians cannot have gained a real victory. On the contrary, they found themselves forced to yield to the Hittites formerly Egyptian spheres of interest all the way to Central Syria.

Although there were no further encounters the state of war—one is tempted to say "the cold war"—lasted fully sixteen years. In addition, the relationship between the two countries was strained by the fact that Murshili III (Urhi-Teshub), the nephew of Hattushili III whom his uncle had dethroned and banished, had fled from his place of exile to Egypt. "When I wrote to him: 'send me my enemy,' he did not send him, and hence I and the king of Egypt were angry with each other," it says in a letter from Hattushili to the Kassite king Kadashman-enlil of Babylon. Nevertheless, in the twenty-first year of Ramesses II, in 1270/69, a treaty was concluded between him and the Hittite Great King, Hattushili III. It was the result of extensive preparations and negotiations and led to a more stable relationship between the two great powers. The treaty guaranteed the *status quo* of their possessions and made provisions for military support in case of an external entanglement of either party. We have about forty-five letters from the archive of Boğazköy concerning both this event and the subsequent developments between the two great countries in the following years. Not only did the two Great Kings take part in this correspondence but also the two queens, the king of the one state writing to the queen of the other and vice versa. Indeed, even the mother of Ramesses, Tuya, and his son, Shutahapshap, crown prince of Egypt, appear among the correspondents. Ramesses wrote as many as twenty-six letters to Hattushili in this connection and thirteen to Hattushili's queen, Puduhepa. The letters are all similar in tenor: they express what relief was brought about by the conclusion of this peace treaty between the two great rival powers. The contents of the treaty were formulated in Akkadian, that is, in the Babylonian idiom which was then current in international diplomacy. We know the contents both from Egypt and from the Hittite capital. The Babylonian wording of the Hittite version was translated into Egyptian and carved in hieroglyphs on the walls of several temples. On the other hand, we also have a cuneiform Akkadian text from Boğazköy, representing the Egyptian version of the treaty. We gather that the originals exchanged between the two chanceries were not written on clay but on silver tablets. From the Egyptian hieroglyphic text we learn that the original document bore a seal of which the description follows:

> What is in the middle of the table of silver. On the front side: a figure consisting of the image of Seth, embracing an image of the Great Prince of Hatti, surrounded by a border inscribed with these words: "the seal of Seth, the ruler of Heaven, the seal of the treaty, which Hattushili made, the Great Prince of Hatti, the mighty, the son of Murshili, the Great Prince of Hatti, the mighty."

This is a remarkably accurate description of the great state seals used by the Hittite kings of the later 14th and the 13th centuries B.C. for the authentication of such official documents. Thanks to the excavations, we have seen such seals from Boğazköy proper, such as one magnificent impression on a clay bulla which was once appended to a tablet (plate 25c). This seal portrays the Great King Muwatalli embraced and guided by his personal god. We also encounter the same motif in monumental Hittite art. We discussed the relief in the rock sanctuary of Yazılıkaya, only a mile outside the Hittite capital, which shows the Great King Tuthaliya IV, son of Hattushili III, similarly embraced and guided by his tutelary god, Sharruma (plate 25a). The figure of the god is rendered larger than that of the king. He not only protects but also guides him on his path, having taken him by the hand.

Thirteen years later, in the thirty-fourth year of the reign of Ramesses II, the conclusion of peace between the two great powers was crowned by an event depicted in an Egyptian relief. It is the marriage of Ramesses to the eldest daughter of the Hittite Great King.

In front of the famous rock temple of Abu Simbel (which has had to be moved and placed on a higher terrace due to the rising water of the new Nile dam) there is a rock-hewn terrace. Adjoining it at the back are the giant colossi of Ramesses II, and between them is the entrance to the rock temple. On the rock face bordering the south side of the terrace there is a weather-beaten relief (plate 26a) portraying, on the left side, the Egyptian king Ramesses II seated between two gods under a canopy. From the right two figures approach with raised hands in a gesture of respectful submission. The figure in front is female, the other is male, attired in a wide cloak and wearing a tall conical hat. By their attire they are unmistakably characterized as non-Egyptians, a fact confirmed by the accompanying hieroglyphic text. It relates extensively that the Hittite Great King Hattushili (III) had come to Egypt to give his daughter in marriage to the pharaoh. The Hittite princess was given the official title of "the Consort of the Great King, Mistress of the two Countries, Mat-nefrure, Daughter of the Great Prince of Hatti." According to the relief in Abu Simbel, the Hittite Great King personally conducted his daughter to Ramesses II and, the inscription says, after a tiresome journey in the winter months. Their destination certainly was not Abu Simbel, for here, in remote Nubia, this event was recorded only because it had created such general interest and satisfaction that it merited portrayal at several sites of Ramesside Egypt. In fact, the encounter and the marriage probably took place at Pi-Ramesses in the eastern Nile delta where the Great King of the 19th Dynasty had his real residence and where he customarily held court.

This dynastic marriage between the Egyptian king and a Hittite princess ended the age-old discord between the two powers. This event is also described to us in unusual detail by letters found in Boğazköy. Envoys of the two courts passed to and fro in order to make preparations for the reception of the princess into the harem of the Egyptian king. There she was not destined to be one among many in the "Women's House" but to have the rank of a chief wife. Finally it was agreed that Egyptian envoys would go to the Hittite capital so that in the name of the pharaoh they would perform the betrothal and receive the royal bride. In a letter written by Ramesses II to Puduhepa, the bride's mother, we read:

> I have seen the tablet my sister has sent me, and I have heard of all the matters about which the Great Queen of Hatti, my sister, has written to me very very beautifully. So speak to my sister: "Behold! The Great King, king of Hatti, my brother, has written to me thus: 'Let people come to pour fine oil on the head of my daughter, and may they take her into the house of the Great King of Egypt!' Thus my brother has written to me. Behold! very, very good is this decision which my brother has written to me about. The Sun God has brought it about, and the Weather God has brought it about, the gods of Egypt and the gods of Hatti have brought about this fine decision to let these two great countries for ever become one single country."

The bride departs under the protection of an envoy sent especially to Hattusha for this purpose. Her royal father gives her a dowry in keeping with her rank consisting not only of precious objects but also of horses and cattle and flocks of sheep. A detachment of troops protects her on her journey. The town of Ramesses in "Canaan" is her first stop in Egyptian territory. The local governor is urged to fulfill his duties towards her with special care.

Nowhere, however, is it mentioned in these texts that the princess was accompanied by her father, the Great King. One was, therefore, always inclined to believe that in the relief of Abu Simbel the Hittite king was represented, as it were, in order to heighten the glory of Ramesses II in the eyes of his countrymen, to make the foreign prince appear like a vassal and a tributary of the Egyptian. Further study of the cuneiform documents found in Boğazköy, however, has recently proved this interpretation to be only partly correct. The relevant evidence comes from two fragments of a letter from Ramesses II to Hattushili III. It was written long after the conclusion of the peace treaty to which it explicitly refers. The letter is only part of an extensive correspondence concerning a matter the beginning of which we can only conjecture from references to letters that are not preserved. It appears that Ramesses II invited the Hittite king to visit him in Egypt. The reply was strangely cool, not to say suspicious, since the Hittite wrote thus: "Would my brother write to me to tell what exactly we should do in Egypt!" Whereupon Ramesses becomes more explicit and repeats the invitation in urgent terms. First he refers to the letter he has received from the Hittite court and answers with some vexation: "What indeed did my brother say!" Then he goes on to say: "The Sun God and the Weather God will make my brother see his brother, and my brother may carry out the good proposal to come to see me, and the one may look the other in the face at the place where the king is seated on his throne. I shall go to the country of Kinahhi (Canaan) to see my brother, to look my brother in the face and to receive him within my country."

Whether the Hittite king actually went on this long journey and met Ramesses at his residence in the eastern delta we do not know. By saying that he will go to the country of Canaan, the Egyptian king means simply that he will go to meet his royal brother in order to welcome and conduct him to his residence. It is quite conceivable that in the representation of the relief the two events which actually followed one another have been telescoped into one and that the visit of the Hittite Great King in fact took place.

"What are we supposed to do in Egypt," asked the Hittite king in his letter. And the Egyptian answered his royal brother: "the one may look the other in the face." This means the establishment of personal contact, as we would call it today. But the underlying idea of Ramesses may have been that such a visit of the ruler of one of the great powers would heighten his glory in his own house and in his country.

In a large inscription of Merenptah, the successor of Ramesses II, it says: "Hatti is in peace." The same Egyptian king helped the country of the Hittites by sending grain when the Hittites suffered from a famine due apparently to a prolonged drought. The grain was sent by boat along the south coast of Asia Minor to a town called Ura. The treaty of the two countries, therefore, proved to be durable and withstood the test also in cases not explicitly foreseen in the text of the treaty. This indicates a *rapprochement* of the two powers exceeding the usual limits. One might even be tempted to infer from the occurrence of names like Mizra-muwa that there were Egyptophile tendencies in Hattusha outside the court.

One has to bear in mind what this *rapprochement* meant. Basically it meant no more and no less than that the two leading states, the Big Two of their time, were in such complete accord that united they could meet any threat from a third party. During the 13th century Assyria slowly gained strength in the east, scoring an occasional success here and there at the expense of the Hittites without being able to assert itself west of the Euphrates. Apparently here the line safeguarded by the Egyptian-Hittite alliance held firm.

And yet this world which seemed so cemented by treaties and friendly relations and, indeed, even by intermarriage between courts proved to be subject to a fate which it could not possibly have foreseen. Barbaric and semibarbaric peoples appeared from outside, invading the civilized world. They arrived from regions beyond its horizon, from southeast Europe, from the Balkan peninsula, and from the Aegean islands, overrunning the coastal areas of southern Asia Minor and irresistibly pushing forward, destroying everything to the gates of Egypt. Ramesses III repulsed them with difficulty in his eighth year, 1191 B.C., and blocked the invasion route into Egypt proper by a land and sea battle somewhere in Southern Syria. He immortalized this decisive event by a frequently quoted inscription carved together with reliefs on the second pylon of the temple of Medinet Habu on the western bank of Thebes. Apart from Egypt, this text lists countries and cities already familiar to us: Carchemish, for instance, which was a Hittite town and, above all, Hattusha itself. In this text Hatti means at least parts of the Anatolian Hittite territory which had fallen prey to the invaders. The inscription of Ramesses III, an Egyptian document, is thus far the only authentic, although indirect, source concerning the fall of an empire which shortly before had maintained its rank as a great power. The empire was dissolved and with it fell its sustaining force, the dynasty of the Great Kings of Hattusha. In the southeast of Anatolia and in northernmost Syria a series of small states arose, some of which endeavored to continue the old Hittite tradition. The former heart of the empire, Central Anatolia, and above all the site of the old capital itself sank into a long period devoid of historical tradition, a truly Dark Age.

VI

HATTUSHA-BOĞAZKÖY IN PHRYGIAN AND PERSIAN TIMES

Hattusha, the capital of the Hittite Empire, was destroyed about 1200 B.C. Büyükkale also, the palace-complex of the Great Kings, was first looted and then so thoroughly destroyed by fire that not a single building remained standing. Moreover, several sculptures, such as gate-lions and gate-bulls, as well as the monumental inscription of King Tuthaliya IV (fig. 24) were deliberately smashed to pieces and thereby deprived of their inherent magic power.

Some scholars have recently suggested that the Hittite capital had been given up and abandoned by its residents because a famine resulting from a long drought forced them to migrate to the southeast, to Southeast Anatolia and North Syria. There is, however, not a shred of evidence for this theory. On the contrary, the evidence for violent enemy action is so flagrant that it cannot be mistaken. Capture, plunder, and arson may have occurred in the way illustrated not by Hittite art, which rarely deals with such profane subject matter, but by a much later Assyrian work, a 7th-century relief from Nineveh (plate 26c). Here we see the capture of the Elamite city Hamanu by the troops of the Assyrian king Ashurbanipal. What takes place in this scene may reflect in a general way what happened at Hattusha.

Records of Great King Shuppiluliuma II are the latest datable entries to have been deposited in the Hittite archives of Boğazköy. This brings us to around 1200 B.C. or shortly afterward. This is also known to be the time when the Hittite Empire was attacked by the so-called Peoples of the Sea. The latter event, known from Egyptian sources, coincides so strikingly with the ceasing of the records in the Hattusha archives that empire and capital evidently perished at about the same time.

The resulting Dark Age in Central Anatolia lasted for over 300 years. Not until the 9th century B.C. do we again encounter historical references. Then this part of Anatolia had come into contact with Assyria. In the years 837 and 836 B.C., the Assyrian king Shalmaneser III received gifts from twenty-four kings of Tabal. A century later, at the time of Tiglath-Pileser III and especially under Sargon II, this Tabal became a unified state under the rule of the dynasty of Burutash. At the time of Sargon, Tabal was located in the area of Kayseri and southward to the Taurus, in the heart of Anatolia. In the east it bordered on Urartu, in the north on Kashku, and in the northwest and west on Mushki. Here we need not deal with the frequent friendly, as well as hostile, contacts between Assyria and Tabal, or with those between Tabal and its Anatolian neighbor states. For our purpose it may suffice to point out that Tabal uses Hittite hieroglyphs for its monumental inscriptions and has other traits which prove it to be an heir of Luvian-Hittite culture. The northernmost Hittite hieroglyphic inscriptions on stone come from Çalapverdi, just to the north of the Halys. As far as we can understand their contents at all, they seem to refer to the later part of the 8th century B.C. Still further to the north, Alişar has yielded seals with the same kind of pictographic writing. I do not, however, think this evidence is strong enough to prove that Tabal extended so far to the north. The Halys River, here running roughly east-west, must in general have been the northern border.

In the cult of Tabal, the goddess Kubaba played an important role as we learn from the local sources. Her cult apparently spread from Carchemish, the ancient seat of her worship, to these parts of Anatolia.

Among the neighbors of Tabal, Kashku and Mushki are of interest. In the case of Kashku, we are dealing undoubtedly with the same ethnic entity which we previously met in the context of events belonging to the second millennium B.C. We came to know them as the never completely pacified northern neighbors of the Hittite Empire. From the Pontic area they repeatedly raided the Hittite lands, at least once even captured the capital, and probably also played a role in the final fall of Hattusha. If we now, in the 8th century B.C., find them so far advanced to the south, all the way from the Halys bend in the west to the upper Euphrates to the east—in an area which had always been the immediate objective of their southward ambitions—we may reasonably interpret this as the result of their successful collaboration in the destruction of Hatti.

In their old habitat, the Pontic mountain range, they had lived during the second millennium as a loose federation of tribes, not ruled by kings. Only once, at the time of the Hittite king Murshili II, do we hear of a Kashkian king, named Pihhuniya, but he is explicitly referred to as an exception occurring "after a time when in Kashka rule by a single man had not existed." The texts concerning the Kashka give us the impression that they followed what has been called a "half-nomadic" routine. It would seem that in the milder season they migrated from their settlements to summer pastures. Their buildings were probably constructed of durable materials but mostly of wood. Houses of this kind, if not set on posts but on wooden thresholds, will not leave any recognizable marks in the soil, so they may tempt the archaeologist into believing that there was a hiatus in occupation whereas in fact this was not the case. It is possible that the Kashka after their migration southward, that is, after 1200 B.C., maintained their native customs and continued to practice their original habitation patterns also in the area of the southern Halys bend. In that case their peculiar kind of architecture would account for the fact that clear traces of settlement are lacking for the period around 1000 B.C.

Some scholars have inferred from the negative evidence that this area was altogether in the hands of roving nomadic tribes who used it for pastures. Such a far-reaching conclusion is difficult to maintain. It has been pointed out that no second-millennium place-names survived the catastrophe of 1200 B.C. in the area of the Halys bend, unlike Southeast Anatolia. Even this offers no real support for the hiatus theory. The name Hattusha may indeed have vanished but our knowledge of Hittite fixed place-names north of the Halys is far too meager to support conclusions of this kind. If the site of Tonea, mentioned by the geographer Ptolemaeus, in the vicinity of modern Alaca is really identical with the old Hittite Taviniya, it might serve as a counterargument.

The Mushki, western and northwestern neighbors of Tabal, have a greater claim to our interest. From at least the middle of the 8th century B.C., they are undoubtedly to be identified with the people we call Phrygians, known also by this name to Homer and later Greek literature. It is equally certain that Mita of Mushki is identical with Midas of the Greek tradition. Mita was a onetime ally of Urartu and Carchemish, a king who had several hostile as well as peaceful contacts with Assyria, mostly in Cilicia. The question remains whether the Mushki of the Assyrian sources are always strictly identical with those Phrygians who according to Greek tradition migrated from Macedonia and Thrace to Asia Minor either before or after the Trojan War. If the answer is positive, we would then know that these Mushki-Phrygians had penetrated far to the Anatolian East, to Kummuh, as early as the time of Tiglath-Pileser I (1115-1077), when the Assyrians repulsed them. On the other had, if we do not equate the Mushki with the Thracians-Phrygians, the name Mushki may be taken as a collective label for northern tribes of various affiliations. In that case the Mushki encountered by Tiglath-Pileser could not simply be interpreted as Phrygians. The name Mita-Midas, of frequent occurrence in Phrygia, is of ancient Anatolian type and is recorded as early as the second millennium B.C.

Regardless of this problem of tribal nomenclature, Phrygia undoubtedly was an important factor at least from the middle of the 8th century B.C. Midas, the son of Gordios, conducted operations in the east either against or with Assyria, at times with Carchemish and Urartu, but also maintained relations with the west. He had married the daughter of the king of Kyme in Aeolis and, according to Herodotus, was the first "barbarian" who sent a votive offering, a throne, to the sanctuary of Apollo in Delphi.

This dynasty had its residence in Gordion on the banks of the Sangarios, the site of intensive and extraordinarily successful excavations by our colleagues from the University Museum in Philadelphia. Their findings convincingly show that the cultural focus of Central Anatolia at that time was at Gordion. The court of the Old Phrygian kings formed the kind of center which in the second millennium had existed east of the Halys at Hattusha. The Kimmerian invasion at the beginning of the 7th century B.C. and the resulting death of Midas apparently did not lastingly affect the central status of Gordion. The archaeological finds prove its continuing importance in the 7th and 6th centuries B.C.

In addition to the Assyrian sources of the 8th century B.C., from the time of kings Tiglath-Pileser III and Sargon II, we also have direct evidence for Phrygian influence east and southeast of the Halys. Five Phrygian alphabetic inscriptions of varying length are known from Hüyük near Alaca; another, shorter inscription is carved near the so-called rock-altar on the hilltop of Kalehisar near Alaca Hüyük. This northern group of inscriptions has a southern counterpart, represented by the so-called Black Stone of Kilisehisar-Tyana, on which the name of Midas occurs. The date of these inscriptions must remain uncertain and their meaning obscure as long as our knowledge of the Old Phrygian language remains as fragmentary as it is at present. Nevertheless, the Black Stone of Tyana is most probably to be dated to the time of Midas, hence to the period of Phrygian activity in Southern Cappadocia and along the borders of Cilicia. This would make the Black Stone contemporary with the earliest Phrygian inscriptions from Gordion.

We have seen that the historical tradition concerning the centuries following the fall of the Hittite Empire is very meager. A long stretch of time, the Dark Age, is completely devoid of records. In the 8th century B.C. it is followed by a period which reveals to us a completely new distribution of territories and power positions as compared to the second millennium B.C. In the area of our interest, the leading elements are Tabal in the south and Mushki-Phrygia in the west. Boğazköy, the old Hattusha, in the later part of the 8th century lies more or less in the border zone between these two. On which side it belonged in the succeeding period is quite obscure. Do the excavation results have an answer for us, and if so, of what kind?

In the vast area of the devastated Hittite capital two places were first reoccupied: the rocky hill Büyükkaya east of the gorge, and Büyükkale. The occupation of Büyükkaya, if we judge by the pottery, may have started a little before that of Büyükkale. Two test cuts have been made on Büyükkaya; they do not as yet give us more details. The situation is different on Büyükkale, where the reoccupation starts with level II, which may be subdivided into two or three sublevels. The earliest constructions were undertaken at a time when the Hittite ruins still lay visible above the surface. On top of them there is no trace of a sterile stratum such as would have been formed by natural sedimentation. This stratigraphic observation as such does not give us a measure of time, but it tends to limit the interval between the end of the Hittite citadel and the beginning of level II. In this layer, and especially in sublevel 2, we found a considerable amount of the kind of pottery which Ekrem Akurgal calls the Early

Phrygian style, dating its acme to the 8th century B.C. I should not like to decide whether this style, as our colleague believes, originated as late as the middle of the 8th century B.C. or rather quite a bit earlier. Nor am I convinced that this style has as yet been conclusively associated with Phrygia and the Phrygians. Both in decoration and in shapes, this class of pottery possesses elements of such strong eastern affinity that I should consider an origin in a non-Phrygian environment much more probable. This pottery of course then may have been taken over in the western part of Central Anatolia by Phrygians. In any case, its occurrence in Boğazköy (fig. 29), and even more so in Alişar, which has indeed yielded outstanding examples of this style of vases, cannot simply be seen as proof that the area within the Halys bend in the 8th century B.C. belonged to the Phrygian orbit.

The Hattusha level in question, level II, must have lasted into

Figure 29. Sherd of vase with deer in "Early Phrygian" style

the beginning of the 7th century B.C., since it contains examples of the black-on-red painted pottery which was mainly popular in the south part of Central Anatolia around Konya.

It is hard to imagine a sharper contrast than that between the Hittite royal citadel of the 13th century and this level II of Büyükkale. Now we have an unfortified, open settlement of small, often single-roomed houses without any noticeable planning (plate 27a). The lower storey in many instances is built as a cellar-like basement, with vertical wooden posts to give strength to the rubble walls. This is in utter contrast to the immediately underlying palace of the Great Kings. Nowhere was the slightest attempt made to reconstruct the Hittite walls and rooms and to put them to better use than that of a handy quarry. The new occupation was by people who in the simplest way settled down in the old ruins, now totally dissociated from the great past. What we said before in an attempt to characterize the Kashku may equally apply to the newcomers in Boğazköy.

Nevertheless, one discovery cautions us not to underestimate the new residents of Boğazköy. Far out from Büyükkale, in a district otherwise unoccupied at this time, directly in front of the great propylon of the precinct of Hittite Temple I, we discovered a small cella, a chapel (fig. 30). The presence of a shrine here can only be interpreted as proof that in spite of the radical change in ethnic and cultural circumstances this particular spot had still maintained some aura of sanctity. The cult-room is small and incompletely preserved. It has benches along its walls, a pedestal in the middle against the back wall, and an offering basin not quite in the center of the room. On the pedestal we found several large votive maceheads, nearby two spearheads of iron and bronze respectively, a small stone eagle, a bronze disc with an embossed design of a lion, an ivory seal with a handle in the shape of an eagle (plate 26b), a painted krater (fig. 31), and a tripod vessel of clay. One of the bowls belonging to the latter vessel has a raised ring around its outer rim, fixed in place with the aid of four crossbars and two spool-shaped handles. This is clearly an imitation in clay of bronze

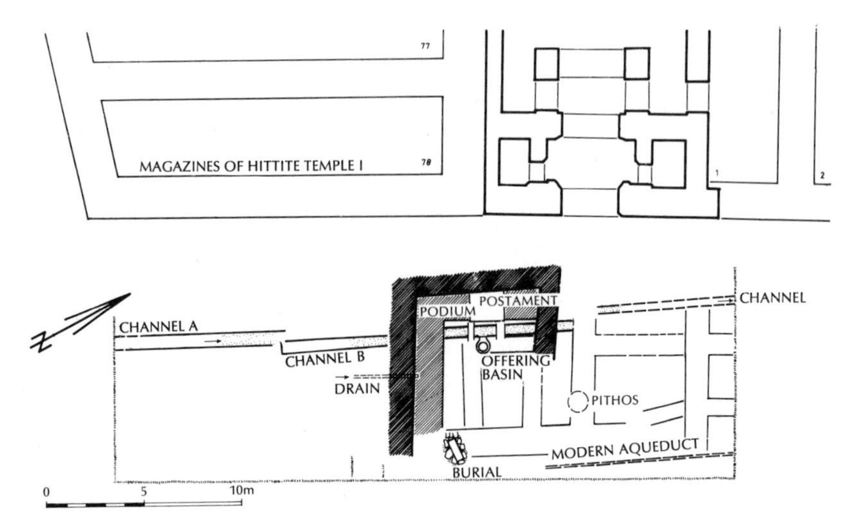

Figure 30. Plan of Phrygian shrine in front of propylon of Temple I

bowls with the same type of handle well known from tumuli at Gordion and also from Ankara. Along with other ceramic finds from the cella, this tripod vase proves that the small shrine

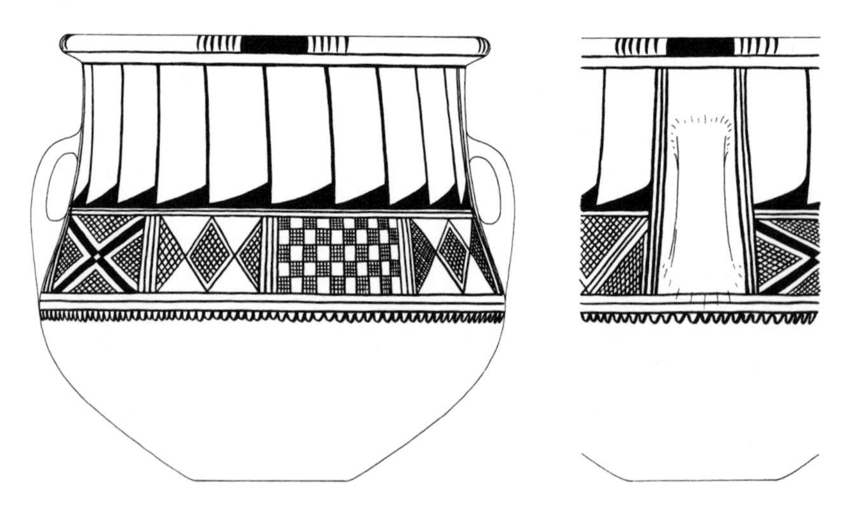

Figure 31. Painted krater from Phrygian shrine. H. 0.359 m

belongs to the late 8th century B.C., as a modest, late descendant of the great Hittite temple, the ruins of which must still have been a striking feature of the site.

Towards the end of the 8th century B.C., Büyükkale saw the erection of some better buildings. A house of 13 meters in length and 8 meters wide is almost perfectly rectangular and constructed with special care. Its door is in the middle of the short south side, and in front of it lies a court with a limestone pavement. A low retaining wall borders this court on three sides. In this building we found a fragment of a large basin-like vessel decorated with a lion in rather high relief, its head projecting above the rim of the vase (fig. 32). The *deinos* has a diameter of about 32

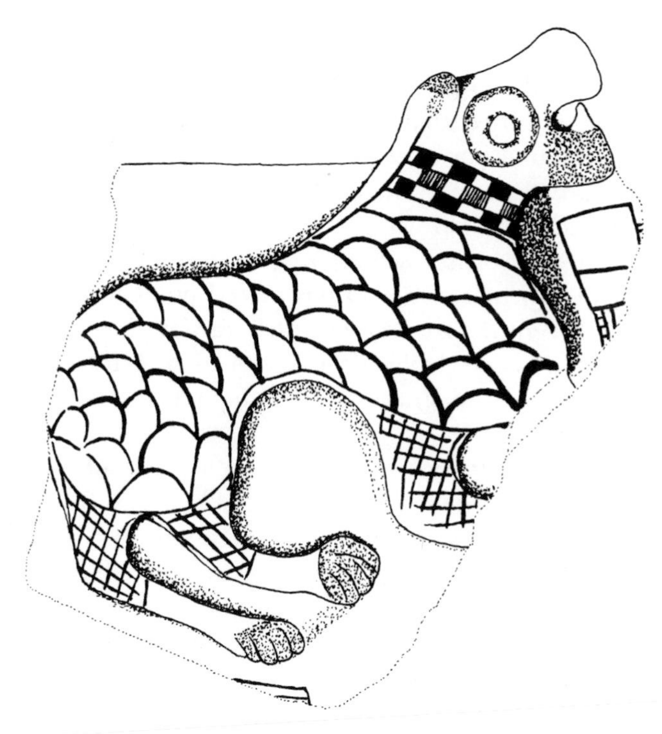

Figure 32. Phrygian vase fragment with lion decoration. L. of lion *ca.* 0.18 m

centimeters, which allows us to restore two more lions along the rim of the vessel, probably facing in the same direction. The lion is painted in red and light brown on a yellow-white ground. Another find from a wall niche in this house was an Assyrian cylinder seal of pink transparent agate. The design shows an adoration scene, with a worshipper at the left facing Ishtar and Sin. The seal must have been made about the middle of the 8th century B.C. Both finds from this building, the lion-*deinos* and the seal, surpass in quality whatever else was brought to light on Büyükkale from both this and the preceding periods. Perhaps this unusual quality is connected with the building and its purpose, which must have been of a special nature. The plan itself is unusual; furthermore, the building stood unaltered at least until about 500 B.C., even while new constructions arose all around it, gradually changing the appearance of Büyükkale. Was the building a small temple?

It has to be admitted that thus far Boğazköy has contributed little to the illumination of what we call the Dark Age. Not a single find has turned up which can be attributed safely to the centuries immediately following the fall of the Hittite capital. The Assyrian seal just discussed and a good deal of pottery which has parallels in Gordion of the Midas period point to the second half of the 8th century B.C. How much earlier the occupation may have been is as yet difficult to determine, but we should emphasize again that the stratigraphic situation does not suggest too long a gap after 1200 B.C.

In the early 7th century B.C., perhaps as a result of the Kimmerian invasion, a fundamental change took place. Büyükkale was provided with a new system of fortifications encircling the plateau of the rocky hill. The interior of the citadel was settled gradually but ended by being completely occupied (fig. 33). In the course of the later 7th century and in the 6th century, the settlement extended beyond Büyükkale and included the adjoining northwest slope, which was also built up, although less intensively, and fortified. For the fortification of the south side an old Hittite defense line was reused; on the north side a new wall was built

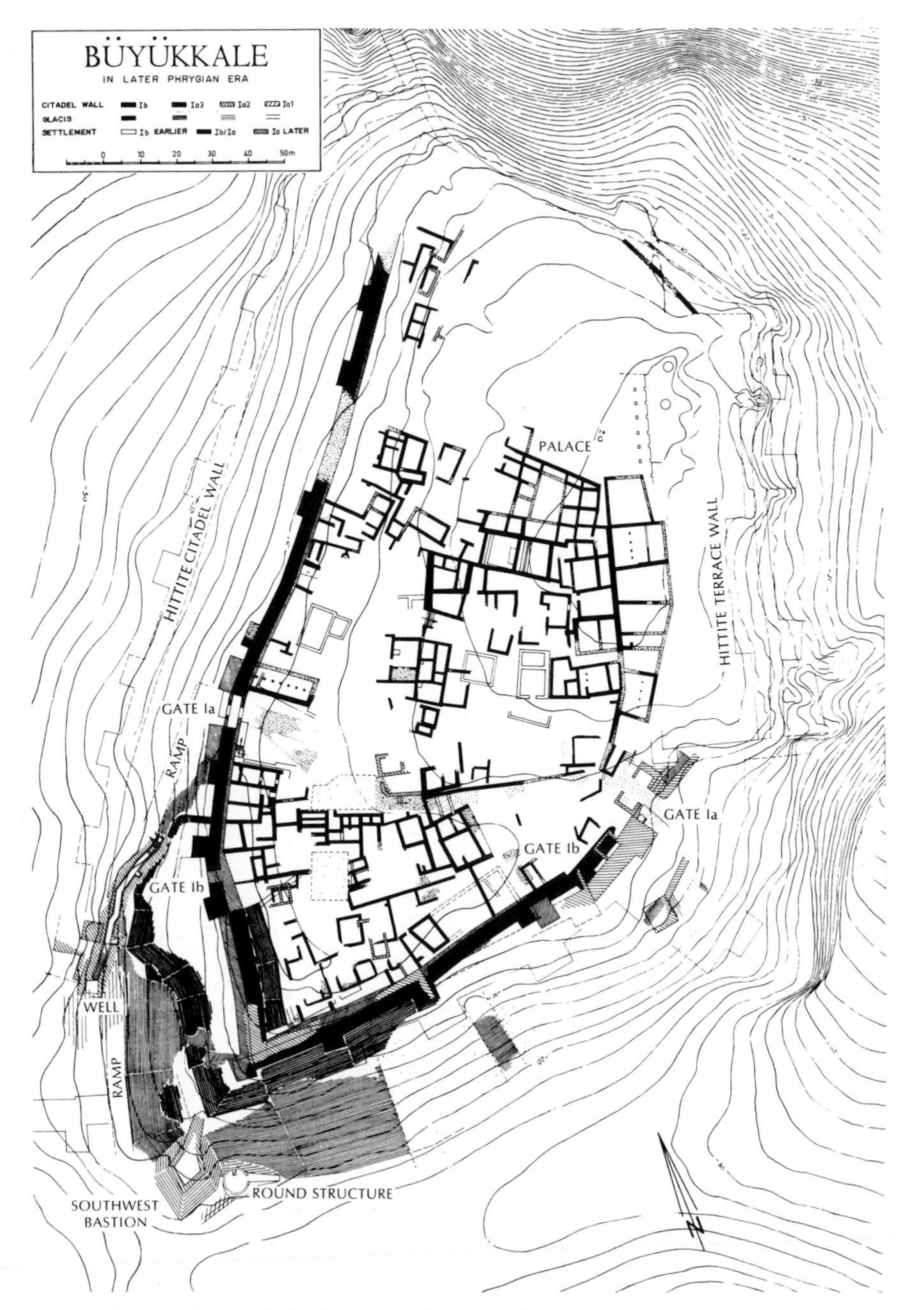

Figure 33. Büyükkale. Plan of Phrygian level I

and provided with towers. Its type of construction follows the modest technique of this period. But even further to the north, outside of the fortified area, single houses and clusters of houses are known to exist. This is particularly true of the area of the so-called House on the Slope, a Hittite building mentioned repeatedly in previous chapters. When we think of Boğazköy we tend to visualize the Hittite city. But the site of the 7th and 6th centuries B.C. is of quite respectable dimensions if compared to other sites of this period, not only in Central Anatolia but also in East Greece of the archaic period. If we recall Larisa in Aeolis and Old Smyrna, or Miletus on the Kalabaktepe in Ionia, it is entirely fair to classify Boğazköy as a *city,* the more so as its inhabited area is at least as large as that of the cities compared.

There is no doubt that this city bore essentially the imprint of Phrygian culture. This is clear from the pottery as well as from many of the architectural features, although there are some differences between Boğazköy and sites west of the Halys, especially in the more prominent city of Gordion. Such differences may be due to the influence of different cultural substrata east of the Halys as opposed to those in the west, in the valley of the Sangarios. The clearest indications of a close connection with Phrygia are given by graffiti in the Phrygian script and language, and above all by cult images, for which we have considerable evidence from Boğazköy. These we will discuss in more detail later on. The combined evidence points to the conclusion that the Phrygian element was predominant at Boğazköy.

The date of the city can be determined best by the imported pottery of western provenance and perhaps also of northern origin, from the Pontic colonies. Local Phrygian pottery is of course found in abundant quantity, but for the time being it is difficult to date in exact terms. The imports from and through East Greece, although limited in quantity, nevertheless allow us to construct a more or less continuous chronology. It starts with proto-Corinthian from the third quarter of the 7th century —the first Greek imports found so far—and a small glazed bottle from the second half of the same century. In addition we have sherds of the East Greek orientalizing style, including some of Milesian fabric. A large *deinos* of local manufacture (fig. 34) is painted with a procession of warriors, in an awkward style yet unmistakably related to East Greek work of the first half of the 6th century B.C. Other native products betray dependence, especially in shapes, on East Greek prototypes of the later part of the 6th century. More recent imports, such as black- or red-figure vases, are totally absent. This may, however, be due to chance. Many of the painted Phrygian vases of the native style show such a laxity in ornament and syntax that one would assign them a lifespan stretching into the 5th century B.C. and perhaps even beyond. The animal ornament on some of these vases rather presupposes Achaemenian inspiration of the 5th century B.C. This would not be surprising in an area which in the 6th century first belonged to the Medes, from the time of Kyaxares on, and then to Achaemenid Persia.

Büyükkale was again the center of a real city. Its architecture is entirely different from that of the Hittites. The fortifications on the south, east, and north sides followed the Hittite layout, as far as we can judge from the preserved remnants. On the west side, however, the Hittite wall stood low on the slope of the citadel and was not reused, evidently because the new builders

Figure 34. Phrygian vase with procession of warriors. H. of frieze *ca.* 0.13 m

could not cope with the technical problems of reconstruction. The new wall and its towers were set much higher up along the slope. The heavy terrace walls of the Hittite buildings E, F, G, and H of Büyükkale were used as the bedding for the new citadel wall. The exploitation of this favorable situation on the other hand necessitated the retrenchment of the southwest corner. The southwest corner tower of Phrygian Büyükkale lies in the outer part of the lower Hittite court, considerably inside the Hittite gate.

In the earlier period there was only one gate on the west side with a rather narrow passageway, with flanking towers and an open area in front. In the 6th century this gate was filled in. Instead, a new gate was built a little to the north. The only innovation in type is to be seen in the introduction of a long, narrow gate-room with two sets of doors. Later still, another gate was built to the southeast (fig. 35). This at first consisted merely of a wide doorway flanked by a single heavy tower. In a later phase the gate was remodeled into a wide chamber with two sets of doors. The open area in front of the gate and the gate chamber itself were paved. One of the pivot stones of the

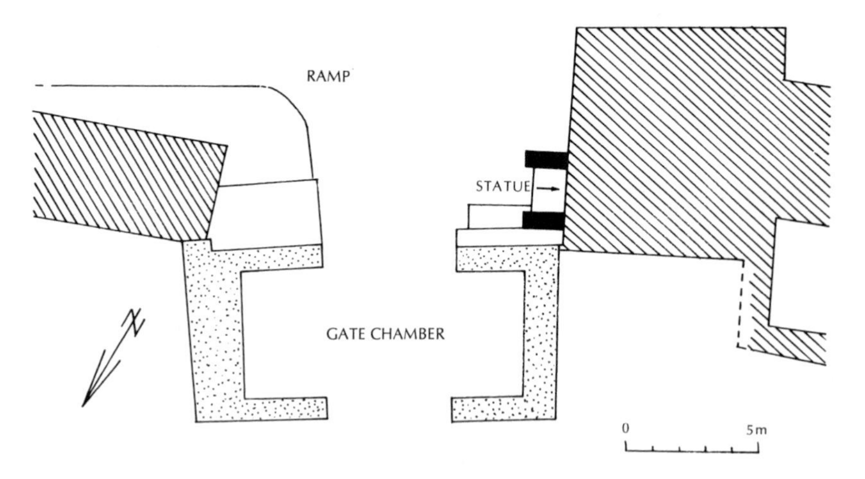

Figure 35. Büyükkale. Plan of Phrygian southeast gate

doorways was still found *in situ*. From the two gates, stone paved or gravel roads led to the interior of the city. All of the gates were set relatively high along the slope, and had to be reached from the low outside level via oblique ramps. These led to artificially terraced open areas in front of the gates proper. The gates themselves belong to a type which is frequently found in Assyria, Northern Syria and in the late Hittite cities of Southeast Anatolia. This type has a strikingly early predecessor in Boğazköy itself, as will be recalled, in the form of a Hittite gate of the 14th century B.C. which lies only a few yards away from these gates of the Phrygian period.

The entire south slope and the southern part of the west slope of Büyükkale were covered with a slanting pavement of limestone (plate 27b) which starts at the foot of the incline and rises all the way up to the citadel wall. Thus, the weakest sides of the fortress hill were harnessed in stone, difficult to scale by the enemy and at the same time protected against erosion by heavy rainstorms and melting snow. This stone glacis underwent several repairs. It was also altered to conform to the shifting of the ramps to the gates on the west side. The last alteration was connected with the erection of a large bastion at the southwest corner of the citadel. This was designed in radiating form, in this respect a striking predecessor of Vauban's constructions of the 17th century of our era. The bastion extended to the base of the southwest corner and served to protect the west as well as the south flank of the citadel.

This stone-paved glacis had its predecessors. The Hittites used them in the 14th and 13th centuries B.C. as we know from Hüyük near Alaca and also from Hattusha itself, where the entire slope in front of the southern city wall near Yerkapı was paved in this manner. The Phrygians apparently imitated prototypes which were still exposed and visible during their time. In the 7th and 6th centuries B.C. this kind of glacis became a typical feature in the architectural fortifications of central and northern Anatolia. In Göllüdağ near Niğde it may occur as early as the 8th century. Later examples are found at Kerkenesdağ, Havuzköy, and Akalan, that is, in Cappadocia and in the Pontic area. And in the citadels of Toprakkale in Cilicia, Til Basher, Aleppo, and Hama in Syria, the same technique, admittedly in more perfect form, also had its applications in the early Middle Ages. In these areas local prototypes provided inspiration for an important architectural element in many crusaders' castles.

In the 6th century, probably after 550 B.C., a cutting was made in the glacis on the west slope to accommodate a long stairway which descends in a crooked course to a well at the base of the hill (plate 28). This stairway has vertical sides, with two niches in the side towards the citadel. The steps of the staircase are carefully laid, with landings at two places. The trapezoidal well-shaft was filled not by a spring but by groundwater which appears even in summer, as we know from experience, and is both clean and good to drink. It trickles through from the interior of the citadel hill where it collects behind a layer of clay. Two of the stone-lined walls of the well-shaft have horizontal inserts of wooden beams. Where the staircase reaches the basin, the beams are set at right angles in a manner which immediately betrays their purpose. They served as supports for a floor of planks, a platform at the end of the staircase to be used by those drawing water from the well.

The lack of springs within the citadel and the seasonal nature of the rain-water supply must have been the reason this staircase and well-shaft were built. But they also implied a risk, for this new water supply lay outside of the fortification walls and even beyond normal bowshot range from the platforms of the towers. To counteract this drawback a tower was built far down the slope beside the staircase, slightly uphill from the well-shaft. This free-standing, square tower was probably of moderate height, but in case of emergency the water supply route and the well-shaft could be defended from its top.

It seems to us that this particular kind of water supply may be seen as belonging to the Phrygian building tradition. It is true that similar, even related arrangements also occur elsewhere and in other periods. But in this case, the situation on the slope of the mountain and the type of descent correspond very closely to staircases and water supply systems in Phrygia proper. The so-called Midas City, not far from the springs of the Sangarios, offers especially pertinent examples. The parallels are close enough to suggest a connection.

If the excavations show a clear picture of the fortifications, gates, towers, bastions, and glacis, this is unfortunately not the case in the interior of the citadel. Building activities in this area were so lively and clearance for new projects so frequent that we can recover no more than an incomplete version of the architecture. We cannot even blame the instigators of the repeated demolitions, since they were clearly people of a parsimonious and economical frame of mind. They were primarily interested in good building material, in neatly cut blocks which could be quarried out of the lower-lying Hittite ruins to be cut and recut in several stages of Phrygian building activities.

In general terms, the former layout can still be recognized. The upper plateau was separated by retaining walls from the lower one to the south and west. From the west, a broad staircase gave access to the upper plateau, whose northern part was occupied by a complex of many rooms apparently with a rectangular courtyard in the center. In this complex we may see the residence of the ruler of Phrygian Boğazköy, but it is not easily classified as a particular or even generally known type of building. A detailed study of the preserved remains is still to be made and may lead to more definite results. Part of this complex (in a wider sense, because it is set within the south enclosure wall) is the building which had remained standing since the end of the 8th century, the one we tentatively identified as a temple. On the east side the entire complex is again shown to be a true unit, since it is bordered there by a heavy, long wall with one change in direction. Several large rooms are built against the outside of this wall; two of these have one cross-wall each, and two have four pillars each as roof supports. A stairway gave direct access to these rooms from the east gate.

If we may see these constructions on the upper plateau as the center of the city complex, as the residential and official quarters of a king of the Phrygian period, we may rank as of lesser importance the other habitation areas on the lower plateau. Even so there are buildings of respectable size among them. One rectangular, single-room house has no fewer than seven pillars along its main axis. Another house, slightly to the south, is also built against the inner face of the citadel wall. This has three rooms set one behind the other, with the entrance in the middle of the short side. Both houses belong to a building type which also appears in the upper, and therefore inner, part of the citadel.

But above all, discoveries of religious significance suggest that we are dealing with an area in close contact with Phrygia during the period discussed. In the southeast gate of the citadel a niche built in the latest phase of the gate contained a statue-group (fig. 36; plate 29). Steps led up to the niche and stone benches flanked it as repositories for votive gifts. A female deity in the center, wearing a tall *polos,* is flanked on either side by a youthful, male figure in short trousers. One of these plays a seven-stringed kithara, the other, who wears a cheekstrap, plays the double flute. In the goddess we may certainly recognize Kubaba-Kybele, for the statue has exactly the traits which point both east and west. Kubaba was at home in the east, especially in Carchemish. Her cult spread from there through Melitene and definitely through Tabal to the west, to Phrygia, where we then meet the goddess in the guise of Kybele. All the essential features of the cult statue of Büyükkale are of eastern imprint, in keeping with the homeland of Kubaba. But the skirt of the goddess, its long border, and especially the manner in which the edge of the garment is tucked in and creates a set of curved folds, betray a clearly western influence. Ultimately this goes back to East Greek art of the 6th century B.C., the most striking example of which is the Samian Hera dedicated by Cheramyes *c.* 560 B.C. This is not surprising, since from the so-called Midas City in Phrygia we have fragments of draped statues which show a much greater dependence upon East Greek art. Cult statues of Kybele from Gordion, Ayaş west of Ankara, and from Ankara itself point to the route along

Figure 36. Phrygian cult niche. Tentative reconstruction

which this influence moved eastward. All of these statues, together with the sculpture from Boğazköy, form a special group of Kybele renderings, in spite of individual minor variations and a strong eastern element in the Boğazköy statue, which is to be expected to the east of the Halys.

The goddess with her companions stood in a niche in the forecourt of the gate and thus outside of the citadel wall. We may look upon her as a guardian of the gate, like Hekate, a concept equally of oriental origin, although quite often adopted in the west. The niche was five feet wide and nearly six feet high, and built of rubble walls with a framework of vertical and horizontal wooden beams. The position of the niche in the corner between the front wall and the jamb of the gate suggests that its roof was not flat, which would have made drainage of rain water awkward, but of gable shape. This detail proves an even closer connection between the Boğazköy cult-statue and Phrygia west of the Halys, where the Kybele of the Ankara relief stands in an aedicula with a typically Phrygian gable. The Gordion Kybele stood in a similar aedicula, to judge by the traces of the gable. Above all, the impressive cult façade of Arslankaya presents Kybele with her two rampant, flanking lions standing in a similar, vastly enlarged niche.

Cult-statues of Kybele-Kubaba like the example from Büyükkale were surely exceptions in the Phrygian part of Cappadocia. On the other hand, there were images of the goddess totally different from the type of cult-statue just discussed. These effigies still preserve the form of ancient idols with disc-shaped or rectangular heads, offset shoulders, and flat body without articulation. They are made of stone; however, many must have been carved of wood and are now lost. A stela of this kind (fig. 37) was found in the north wing of the gate-room of the same gate which had the cult-statue. Both images ended up in burned debris after a destruction to be dated at the latest about 500 B.C. They were originally set up in close proximity to each other. Other idols of this kind were not infrequent in the fill of contemporary Boğazköy. Such stelae in idol form were also known in Hittite times, an example comes from the complex of Temple I in the northern part of the city. It is also probable that the so-called huwashi- and zi-kini-stones which played such an important role in the Hittite cult were aniconic or semi-iconic stelae of this kind. There may even have been an old, local tradition which preserved the appeal of such εἴδωλα. But in the specific form discussed here, they have their counterparts in Phrygia proper; there are numerous examples in Gordion, as I learned through the kindness of the excavators: an example from Fahared Çeşme west of Ankara; and at least two examples from the so-called Midas City. The examples from Fahared Çeşme and Midas City are double idols, perhaps representing Kybele

Figure 37. Schematic idol from north chamber of Phrygian gate. H. 0.299 m, W. of lower edge 0.21 m

and Attis. Some of these stelae have spiral curls on either side of the head, implying that the representation is female. The same locks occur on the goddess of the great cult-statue, as we noticed, and we also see them in a design on a painted 6th-century *deinos* from Büyükkale (fig. 38). Here a female figure in a long dress reaching to the ground places her hands on two antithetical lions. In meaning this scene does not differ from that of the giant monument of Arslankaya. Undoubtedly we should interpret all of these images—primitive, abstract, and fully anthropomorphic—as renderings of Kybele. Thus we learn that Boğazköy at this time had strongly Phrygian leanings in religious art.

In addition to the *naiskos* in front of the gate and the potential temple in the interior of the citadel (the 8th-century building which was so carefully kept intact), we have a third construction which may belong in the same category. As one of the last projects,

Figure 38. Phrygian vase design with goddess and lions. Maximum preserved height 0.1915 m

a strange round construction was erected outside of Büyükkale, directly to the east of the southwest bastion (plate 30). The paving of the glacis was removed here, the building was then constructed, and finally a new pavement was fitted around it. The structure forms a high platform of almost perfect circular shape. It was fitted together out of neatly cut sandstone blocks and has a battered outer face. A slanting ramp gives access to it from the east. The top surface is bordered by a rather low parapet with semicircular coping stones. The entrance from the ramp is framed by limestone blocks to the left and right. On the side towards the citadel hill the platform has a sandstone pedestal which undoubtedly once served as the base for an altar or a sizable statue now completely lost. We know of no similar or even related complex which might help in the interpretation of the present arrangement. I should think it almost certain that this was a cult-place for ceremonies performed by a priest on top of the platform, while the worshippers congregated down below in the depression south of Büyükkale.

We have, then, a fairly clear picture of Boğazköy in the first half of the first millennium B.C. except for the earliest phase. The settlement represented by Büyükkale II lasted from at least the 8th century B.C. and perhaps from considerably earlier times, to the beginning of the 7th century. We cannot yet tell whether Büyükkale II was already in Phrygian hands and inhabited by Phrygians. In the present state of the evidence, basing our conclusions on other sites as well as on Boğazköy, we must also admit the possibility that this area could still have been dominated by tribes and federations of tribes which had participated in the extinction of the Hatti Empire and the destruction of Hattusha. In the bend of the Halys we would first of all think of the Kashka, a tribe which disappears from the Assyrian records after Sargon II. This may give us the 8th century B.C. as the approximate time when the Phrygian element, after various preliminary attempts, came to prevail east of the Halys. But Boğazköy must certainly have been Phrygian in the later 7th century, in the 6th, and even in part of the 5th century B.C. on the evidence of its architecture and pottery and particularly on the evidence of the dominant cult. It was, moreover, a city with a citadel on Büyükkale which must have been the residence of a dynastic family of some rank. Was this a dynasty of merely local importance or did its authority extend beyond the immediate vicinity? Is there a name in the ancient historical tradition which might be associated with this sizable community?

In the course of the 7th century B.C. southeastern Asia Minor had vanished from the horizon of the Assyrians, Tabal about the middle of the century, Cilicia about a quarter of a century later. Thus ends the information from the Assyrian side. Historically speaking, this part of Asia Minor again enters a Dark Age, illuminated only by rare data, some from the Babylonian, some from the early Greek historians, concerning the establishment of the Halys as the borderline between the Medes and Lydia in 585 B.C., the military campaign of Croesus to Cappadocia, and his defeat by Cyrus in 547 B.C. The invasion by Croesus of the area east of the Halys destroyed the land of the Pterians and conquered and subjugated their city which was called Pteria. The land of the Pterians, according to Herodotus, was the most powerful part of Cappadocia and lay κατὰ Σινώπην. Herodianus accordingly called Pteria a πόλις Σινώπης καὶ Μήδων. Κατά can here hardly have the meaning "near" Sinope, but it rather must mean "in line with" Sinope, "on the meridian of" Sinope. The city of Sinope lies considerably to the west of the lower course and the estuary of the Halys. A city and a district east of the river then cannot possibly have been near Sinope. Herodotus apparently referred to Sinope because this old Milesian colony and its whereabouts were familiar to the Greeks and thus could well serve as a topographical aid to locate a district in the interior, within the bend of the Halys which curves far out to the west. It is also much more probable that the encounter in the land of the Pterians and the battle between Croesus and Cyrus, who had crossed the Tigris between the upper and lower Zab in April 547 and then turned west, was fought not in the distant coastal zone of the Pontus, but farther to the south, in the interior of the country. Such a location for Pteria also fits the invasion route from the west, from Lydia, which would have naturally been followed by Croesus. On these grounds Boğazköy used to be equated with Pteria in the days when the date of the ruins had not yet been analyzed. When indisputable evidence proved Boğazköy to be the capital of the Hittite Empire, Pteria seemed to be eliminated. Attempts have been made to locate it elsewhere. Amasya, Akalan, Kerkenesdağ have been considered as candidates. A few scholars continued to opt for Boğazköy. I was not of their opinion because it seemed to me that Boğazköy showed insufficient importance during the historical period in question. But excavation has recently revealed a city complex of considerable dimensions for the 7th and 6th centuries B.C. Hence it becomes not improbable after all that the old Hattusha was known as Pteria in Phrygian and Median times and was identical with the city occupied by Croesus, taken over by Persian rule, and preserved in history by Herodotus.

In all this Yazılıkaya, the old gallery of Hittite rock reliefs of the 13th century B.C. may have played a major role. We have seen that Yazılıkaya did not totally decline after the fall of the densely settled Hittite capital. It is true that the built constructions fell into ruins and gradually disappeared, but the reliefs of the gods remained as they were, almost undamaged. Whatever damage is evident now was almost entirely caused by nature, hardly at all by human hands. In spite of all the radical changes in the political and probably also ethnic domain, the newcomers were not so far removed from their predecessors of the second millennium B.C. in the religious domain that at least the principal figures of the great procession of gods could not also have had an appropriate meaning to them. The finds show that the rock chambers continued to be visited. There is pottery from the 7th and 6th centuries and one vase from the side chamber represents a rare shape of the 7th century. During the excavations in the fall of 1966, we found a burial in one of the niches located in the back face of the rock which carries the main scene of the great divine procession on its inner surface. This burial was accompanied by a cylinder seal, unusual as such in this area, and undoubtedly of the Achaemenian period. Thus, even the second purpose of the rock chambers, their use as burial grounds, was preserved or at least revived in this late period. The rock reliefs, which had a meaning for people of the most diverse languages, and appealed to their imagination, may have been the main reason Boğazköy continued to attract settlers.

These chapters have sketched, in its main features, the role of Hattusha in history, culture, and cult. In the second millennium the history of Hattusha is a mirror of the history of Anatolia, and at times even of North Syria and Upper Mesopotamia; while in the first half of the first millennium it at least reflects the history of Central Anatolia. Then Hattusha is eclipsed by other sites which, due to internal or external circumstances, proved to be more accessible to the influences now entering in gradually increasing strength from the Hellenic West and from the Pontic area in the north. The site sank into insignificance, until excavations in our era and the interpretation of the results awakened it to a new life and re-created before our eyes its great past.

BIBLIOGRAPHY

CHAPTER I

Texier, Charles. *Description de l'Asie Mineure* (Paris, 1839), Vol. I, pp. 209ff.

Sterrett, J. R. Sitlington. "An Epigraphical Journey in Asia Minor" (*Papers of the American School of Classical Studies at Athens,* Vol. II, 1883-84, pp. 308ff.)

Wright, W. *The Empire of the Hittites* (London, 1884; second edition, 1886).

Sayce, A. H. "The Monuments of the Hittites" (*Transactions of the Society of Biblical Archaeology,* Vol. 7, 1882, pp. 248-93).

Sayce, A. H. *The Hittites: The Story of a Forgotten Empire* (London, 1888; fifth and last edition, 1910).

Chantre, Ernest. *Mission en Cappadoce 1893-1894* (Paris, 1898).

Schäffer, E. "Die Ruinen von Boghas-köi" (*Mitteilungen des Kaiserlich Deutschen Archaeologischen Instituts,* Athenische Abteilung, Vol. XXX, 1895, pp. 451-65).

Winckler, Hugo. "Vorläufige Nachrichten über die Ausgrabungen in Boghaz-köi im Sommer 1907" (*Mitteilungen der Deutschen Orient-Gesellschaft* No. 35, 1907, pp. 1-59).

Puchstein, Otto. *Boghasköi, Die Bauwerke* (Leipzig, 1912. *Wissenschaftliche Veröffentlichungen der Deutschen Orient-Gesellschaft,* No. 19=*WVDOG* 19).

Excavation Reports of the expedition from 1931 on:

Mitteilungen der Deutschen Orient-Gesellschaft (=*MDOG*) Nos. 70 (1932); 72 (1933) to 78 (1940); 86 (1953) to 89 (1957); 91 (1958); 93 (1962) to 95 (1965); 97 (1966); 101 (1969).

Boğazköy I: Kurt Bittel and Hans Gustav Güterbock. *Boğazköy. Neue Untersuchungen in der hethitischen Hauptstadt* (Abhandlungen der Preussischen Akademie der Wissenschaften, Philosophisch-Historische Klasse, 1935, 1).

Boğazköy II: Kurt Bittel and Rudolf Naumann. *Boğazköy II. Neue Untersuchungen hethitischer Architektur* (Abhandlungen der Preussischen Akademie der Wissenschaften, Philosophisch-Historische Klasse, 1938, 1).

Boğazköy III: Kurt Bittel, Rudolf Naumann, Thomas Beran, Rolf Hachmann, Gottfried Kurth. *Boğazköy III. Funde aus den Grabungen 1952-1955* (Berlin, 1957).

Güterbock, Hans G. "New Excavations at Boğhazköy, Capital of the Hittites" (*Archaeology,* Vol. 6, 1953, pp. 211-16).

Final Publications:

Boğazköy-Hattusa. Ergebnisse der Ausgrabungen des Deutschen Archaeologischen Instituts und der Deutschen Orient-Gesellschaft Vol. I (Stuttgart 1952), Vol. II (Berlin 1958), Vol. III (Berlin 1963), Vol. IV (Berlin 1963), Vol. V (Berlin 1967), Vol. VI (Berlin 1969) =*WVDOG* Nos. 63, 71, 74-76, 81.

Essential Editions of Hittite Cuneiform Texts:

Keilschrifturkunden aus Boghazköi (=*KUB*) I-XXXIX (Berlin, 1921-63).

Keilschrifttexte aus Boghazköy (=*KBo*) 1-16 (Berlin, 1916-68).

Hittite Hieroglyphic Inscriptions:

Laroche, Emmanuel. *Les Hiéroglyphes Hittites* (Paris, 1960), Vol. 1.

Hittite History:

Goetze, Albrecht. *Kleinasien* (Handbuch der Altertumswissenschaft III, I, 3; Munich, 1957), pp. 84ff.

Schmökel, Hartmut. *Hethitische Geschichte* (Handbuch der Orientalistik II, 3, Leyden 1957), pp. 119-53.

Gurney, O. R. *The Hittites* (Penguin Books, revised edition, 1964).

The Cambridge Ancient History:

Fasc. 40. Lewy, Hildegard. *Anatolia in the Old Assyrian Period* (Cambridge, 1965).

Fasc. 11. Gurney, O. R. *Anatolia c. 1750-1600 B.C.* (Cambridge, 1962).

Fasc. 44. Gurney, O. R. *Anatolia c. 1600-1380 B.C.* (Cambridge, 1966).

Fasc. 37. Goetze, A. *Anatolia from Shuppiluliumash to the Egyptian War of Muwatallish. The Hittites and Syria 1300-1200 B.C.* (Cambridge, 1965).

Otten, Heinrich. "Hethiter, Hurriter und Mitanni" (*Fischer Weltgeschichte. Die Altorientalischen Reiche* II. Frankfurt, 1966), pp. 102-76.

Archives and Libraries at Hattusha:

Laroche, E. "La Bibliothèque de Hattusa" (*Archiv Orientálni,* Vol. XVII, 1949, pp. 7-23).

Otten, Heinrich. "Bibliotheken im Alten Orient" *(Das Altertum,* Vol. I, 1955, pp. 67-81).

CHAPTER II

Hittite Architecture and Town Building in General:

Frankfort, Henri. *The Art and Architecture of the Ancient Orient* (The Pelican History of Art, 1954), pp. 117ff.

Naumann, Rudolf. *Architektur Kleinasiens von ihren Anfängen bis zum Ende der hethitischen Zeit* (Tübingen, 1955).

Early Habitation Levels at Büyükkale and in the Town:

MDOG No. 93 (1965), pp. 27ff. (P. Neve); No. 97 (1966), pp. 16ff. (P. Neve); *WVDOG* 74 (=*Boğazköy-Hattusa* III, W. Orthmann); *WVDOG* 81 (=*Boğazköy-Hattusa* VI, W. Schirmer), pp. 36ff.

The Settlement of the Old Assyrian Period:

MDOG No. 89 (1957), pp. 6ff.; *MDOG* 91 (1958), pp. 17ff. (P. Neve).

Old Assyrian Tablets:

MDOG No. 89 (1957), pp. 68ff. (H. Otten).

Balkan, Kemal. *Observations on the Chronological Problems of the Karum Kanis* (Ankara, 1955).

Balkan, Kemal. *Letter of King Anum-Hirbi of Mama to King Warshama of Kanish* (Ankara, 1957).

Garelli, Paul. *Les Assyriens en Cappadoce* (Paris, 1963).

Fischer, Franz. *"Boğazköy und die Chronologie der altassyrischen Handelsniederlassungen in Kappadokien"* (*Istanbuler Mitteilungen* 15, 1965, pp. 1-16; important contribution).

Tablet of King Anitta:

MDOG No. 83 (1951), p. 39-45 (H. Otten).

Tablet of Hattushili I:

MDOG No. 91 (1958), pp. 75-84 (H. Otten). Important Reviews: Goetze, A. in *Journal of Cuneiform Studies* 16 (1962), pp. 24-30; Güterbock, H. G. in *Journal of Cuneiform Studies* 18 (1964), pp. 1-6,

Letter of Kashshu to the King:

MDOG No. 97 (1966), pp. 13.

Temples in the Upper City:

Krause, Karl. *Boğazköy Tempel V, ein Beitrag zum Problem der hethitischen Baukunst* (Berlin, 1940), especially pp. 56-70.

Residential Quarter in the Lower City:

MDOG No. 91 (1958), pp. 4ff. (P. Neve).

Hazannu, the Burgomaster:

Otten, Heinrich. "Aufgaben eines Bürgermeisters in Hattusa" (*Baghdader Mitteilungen,* Vol. 3, 1964, pp. 91-95).

CHAPTER III

The So-called MESHEDI Tablet:

Jacob-Rost, Liane. "Beiträge zum hethitischen Hofzeremoniell"

(*Mitteilungen des Instituts für Orientforschung,* Vol. 11, 1965, pp. 165-225). Preliminary edition and translation.

The Physical Appearance of the Hill of Büyükkale:
WVDOG 63 (=*Boğazköy-Hattusa* I), pp. 37ff.

City-Gate just below Büyükkale:
MDOG No. 97 (1966), pp. 64ff.

Courts and Pillar-Halls of Büyükkale:
MDOG No. 95 (1965), pp. 14ff.; No. 97 (1966), pp. 14ff.

Audience Hall:
Boğazköy III, pp. 10ff.

Findspots of Cuneiform Tablets on Büyükkale (Archives):
MDOG No. 72 (1933), pp. 12ff. and 37-42 (H. G. Güterbock); No. 91 (1958), pp. 57ff. *Boğazköy* II, pp. 17ff. *WVDOG* 63 (=*Boğazköy-Hattusa* I) pp. 53ff.

Transfer of the Seat of the Court to Dattashsha:

Goetze, Albrecht. *Hattusilis, der Bericht über seine Thronbesteigung nebst den Paralleltexten* (Leipzig, 1925) pp. 46-47, 111.

Goetze, Albrecht. *Neue Bruchstücke zum grossen Text des Hattusilis und den Paralleltexten* (Leipzig, 1930), pp. 46-47.

Tablet Reference to the Burning of the Palace of Hatti:
Journal of Cuneiform Studies, Vol. 17, 1963, pp. 88 (W. Helck).

Stamped Clay Bullae and Royal Seals in Building D of Büyükkale:

Güterbock, Hans Gustav. "Das Siegeln bei den Hethitern" (*Symbolae Paulo Koschaker Dedicatae,* Leiden, 1939, pp. 26-36).

Güterbock, Hans Gustav. *Siegel aus Boğazköy,* Vol. I, (Berlin, 1940); Vol. II (Berlin, 1942).

Bittel, Kurt. "Bemerkungen zu dem auf Büyükkale (Boğazköy) entdeckten hethitischen Siegeldepot" (*Jahrbuch für Kleinasiatische Forschung,* Vol. 1, 1950, pp. 164-73).

The End of Hatti:

Otten, H. "Neue Quellen zum Ausklang der hethitischen Geschichte" (*MDOG* No. 94 (1963), pp. 1-23).

Güterbock, H. G. "The Hittite Conquest of Cyprus Reconsidered" (*Journal of Near Eastern Studies,* Vol. 26, 1967, pp. 73-81). Important contribution.

CHAPTER IV

Bittel, Kurt; Naumann, Rudolf; Otto, Heinz. *Yazılıkaya. Architektur, Felsbilder, Inschriften und Kleinfunde* (Leipzig, 1941, = *WVDOG* 61).

Laroche, Emmanuel. "Le Panthéon de Yazılıkaya" *(Journal of Cuneiform Studies,* Vol. 6, 1952, pp. 115-23).

Bittel Kurt; Herre, Wolf; Otten, Heinrich; Röhrs, Manfred; Schäuble, Johann. *Die hethitischen Grabfunde von Osmankayası* (Berlin, 1958, *WVDOG* 71=*Boğazköy-Hattusa* II).

Güterbock, H. G. "Yazılıkaya" (*MDOG* No. 86 (1953), pp. 65-76).

Otten, Heinrich. "Das Felsheiligtum von Yazılıkaya" (*Das Altertum,* Vol. 2, 1956, pp. 141-50).

Otten, Heinrich. "Die Götter von Yazılıkaya" (*Anatolia,* Vol. 4, 1959, pp. 27-37).

Beran, Thomas. "Zum Datum des Felsreliefs von Yazılıkaya" (*Zeitschrift für Assyriologie,* N.F., Vol. 23, 1966, pp. 258-73).

Hittite Polychrome Relief Vases:

Özgüç, Tahsin. "The Bitik Vase" (*Anatolia,* Vol. 2, 1957, pp. 57-78).

Seal of Tuthaliya IV from Ras Shamra:

Schaeffer, Claude F.-A. *Ugaritica* III (Paris, 1956), pp. 14ff., figs. 24, 26 and pl. III-IV; pp. 111ff. (E. Laroche).

Otten, Heinrich. "Ein Text zum Neujahrsfest aus Boğazköy" (*Orientalistische Literaturzeitung,* Vol. 51, 1956, pp. 101-5).

Güterbock, Hans G. "An Outline of the Hittite AN-TAH-SUM-Festival" (*Journal of Near Eastern Studies,* Vol. 19, 1960, pp. 80-89).

Otten, Heinrich. "Eine Beschwörung der Unterirdischen aus Boğazköy" (*Zeitschrift für Assyriologie,* N.F., Vol. 20, 1961, pp. 114-57).

Güterbock, Hans G. "A Votive Sword with Old Assyrian Inscription" (*Studies in Honor of Benno Landsberger on his 75th Birthday, April 21, 1965,* Chicago, 1965, pp. 197f.).

CHAPTER V

Alabaster Vase from Büyükkale:

MDOG No. 70 (1932), p. 20.

Statuette of Sitsneferu:

Bulletin of the Metropolitan Museum of Art, New York, Vol. 16, 1921, pp. 209f. with illustration.

Statuette of Keri, from Kırıkkale:

Von der Osten, H. H., and Allen, T. George. "The Ancient Settlement in Kürigin Kaleh in Asia Minor" (*American Journal of Semitic Languages and Literatures,* Vol. 43, 1927, pp. 293-96 with figs. 11-14).

Allen, T. George. "A Middle Kingdom Egyptian Contact with Asia Minor" (Oriental Institute Publications V, Chicago, 1929, pp. 66f.).

Bone Plaque with Figure of Bes, from Alaca Hüyük:

Koşay, Hâmit Zübeyr. *Ausgrabungen von Alaca Höyük 1936* (Ankara, 1944), p. 60, No. AL/A 88.

Bone Plaque with Djed-Pillar, from Alaca Hüyük:

Arık, Remzi Oğuz. *Les Fouilles d'Alaca Höyük 1935* (Ankara, 1937) pl. 59, No. Al. 63.

Fragment of Red Granite Stela from Büyükkale:

MDOG No. 76 (1938), p. 18, fig. 5.

Obsidian Vase with the Name of the Hyksos King Khyan from Boğazköy:

Stock, Hanns. "Der Hyksos Chian in Boğazköy" (*MDOG* No. 94 (1963), pp. 73-80).

General Comments:

Smith, W. Stevenson. *Interconnections in the Ancient Near East, A Study of the Relationships between the Arts of Egypt, the Aegean and Western Asia* (New Haven, London, 1965).

Helck, Wolfgang. *Die Beziehungen Ägyptens zu Vorderasien im 3. und 2. Jahrtausend v. Chr.* (Wiesbaden, 1962).

Historical References:

Güterbock, Hans Gustav. "The Deeds of Shuppiluliuma as Told

by His Son, Murshili II" (*Journal of Cuneiform Studies,* Vol. 10, 1956, pp. 41-130).

Güterbock, H. G. "Mursili's Accounts of Suppiluliuma's Dealings with Egypt" (*Revue Hittite et Asianique,* Vol 18, fasc. 66-67, 1960, pp. 57-63).

Vergote, J. *Toutankhamon dans les archives hittites* (Istanbul, 1961).

Kuentz, C. "La bataille de Qadech" (*Mémoires de l'Institut Français d'Archéologie Orientale,* Vol. 55, 1934, pp. 81-398).

Hattushili on Muwatalli's War against Egypt:

Pritchard, James B. *Ancient Near Eastern Texts relating to the Old Testament* (Princeton, 1950) p. 319 (A. Goetze).

Edel, Elmar. "K.Bo I 15+19, ein Brief Ramses II. mit einer Schilderung der Kadesschlacht" (*Zeitschrift für Assyriologie,* N.F., Vol. 15, 1950, pp. 195-212).

Helck, Wolfgang. "Urhi-Tesup in Ägypten" (*Journal of Cuneiform Studies,* Vol. 17, 1963, pp. 87-97).

Treaty between Hattushili III and Ramesses II:

Pritchard, James B. *Ancient Near Eastern Texts relating to the Old Testament* (Princeton, 1950), p. 201-3 (Albrecht Goetze).

Breasted, James Henry. *Ancient Records of Egypt,* Vol. III (Chicago, third edition, 1927), pp. 163-174, paragraphs 367-91.

Marriage of Ramesses II and Hittite Princess:

Edel, Elmar. "KUB III 63, ein Brief aus der Heiratskorrespondenz Ramses' II." (*Jahrbuch für Kleinasiatische Forschung,* Vol. 2, 1952-53, pp. 262-73.

Edel, Elmar. "Weitere Briefe aus der Heiratskorrespondenz Ramses' II" (*Geschichte und Altes Testament. Beiträge zur historischen Theologie* 16, 1953) pp. 29-63.

Edel, Elmar. "Die Rolle der Königinnen in der ägyptisch-hethitischen Korrespondenz von Boğazköy" (*Indogermanische Forschungen,* Vol. 60, 1952, pp. 72-85).

The Marriage Stela in Abu Simbel:

Breasted, James Henry. *Ancient Records of Egypt,* Vol. III (Chicago, third edition, 1927), p. 182 ff., paragraphs 415 ff.

Edel, Elmar. "Der geplante Besuch Hattusili's in Ägypten" (*MDOG* No. 92 (1960), pp. 15-20).

CHAPTER VI

Naster, P. *L'Asie Mineure el l'Assyrie aux VIIIe et VIIe siècles av. J.-C.* (Louvain, 1938).

Landsberger, Benno. *Sam'al. Studien zur Entdeckung der Ruinenstätte Karatepe* (Ankara, 1948).

Luckenbill, Daniel David. *Ancient Records of Assyria and Babylonia. Historical Records of Assyria from the Earliest Times to Sargon,* Vol. I (Chicago, 1926), Vol. II (Chicago, 1927).

Schuler, Einar von. *Die Kaskäer, ein Beitrag zur Ethnographie des alten Kleinasien* (Berlin, 1965).

Mellink, Machteld J. (ed.). *Dark Ages and Nomads c. 1000 B.C.* (Uitgaven van het Historisch-Archaeologisch Instituut te Istanbul, Vol. 18, 1964).

Mellink, Machteld J. "Mita, Mushki and the Phrygians" (*Anadolu Araştırmaları,* H. Th. Bossert Memorial Volume, Istanbul 1965).

Ruge, W., and Friedrich, J. *Phrygia* (Topography, Language, History). (Pauly-Wissowa, Vol. 20, 1, 1941, pp. 781ff.).

Barnett, R. D. *Phrygia and the Peoples of Anatolia in the Iron Age (Cambridge Ancient History,* fasc. 56, Cambridge, 1967).

Houwink ten Cate, Ph. H. J. *Kleinasien zwischen Hethitern und Persern (Fischer Weltgeschichte* IV, *Die Altorientalischen Reiche* III, pp. 112ff. Frankfurt, 1967).

Gordion Excavation Reports:

Körte, Gustav and Alfred. *Gordion. Ergebnisse der Ausgrabungen im Jahre 1900 (Jahrbuch des Kaiserlich Deutschen Archäologischen Instituts,* Ergänzungsheft V, Berlin, 1904).

Young, Rodney S. in: *American Journal of Archaeology,* Vol. 59 (1955), pp. 1ff.; Vol. 60 (1956), pp. 249ff.; Vol. 61 (1957), pp. 319ff.; Vol. 62 (1958), pp. 139ff.; Vol. 64 (1960), pp. 227ff.; Vol. 66 (1962), pp. 153ff.; Vol. 68 (1964), pp. 279ff.; Vol. 70 (1966), pp. 267ff.

Friedrich, Johannes. *Kleinasiatische Sprachdenkmäler* (Berlin, 1932), pp. 123-40: Phrygische Texte.

Haas, Otto. *Die phrygischen Sprachdenkmäler* (Sofia, 1966).

Akurgal, Ekrem. *Phrygische Kunst* (Ankara, 1955).

Houses of Level II of Büyükkale:
WVDOG 63 (=Boğazköy-Hattusa I), pp. 72ff.

Iron Age Shrine near Temple I:
MDOG No. 94 (1963), pp. 32-52 (Th. Beran).

Assyrian Cylinder Seal from Büyükkale:
Beran, Thomas. "Fremde Rollsiegel von Boğazköy" (*Vorderasiatische Archäologie. Studien und Aufsätze Anton Moortgat zum 65. Geburtstag gewidmet,* Berlin, 1964, pp. 27ff. with figure).

Imported Pottery in Phrygian Boğazköy:
MDOG No. 94 (1963), pp. 53-71 (E.-M. Bossert).

Phrygian Fortifications and Glacis of Büyükkale, Staircase and Well in the West Slope of Büyükkale:
MDOG No. 97 (1966), pp. 49-57 (P. Neve).

Houses of Level I of Büyükkale:
Boğazköy III, pp. 8f. with figs.

Statue Group in the Southeast Gate of Büyükkale:
MDOG No. 91, 1958, pp. 61ff.
Bittel, Kurt. "Phrygisches Kultbild aus Boğazköy" (*Antike Plastik* Lieferung II, Teil I, Berlin, 1963).
Laroche, Emmanuel. "Koubaba, Déesse Anatolienne, et le problème des origines de Cybèle" (*Eléments Orientaux dans la Religion Grecque Ancienne,* Paris, 1960, pp. 113-28).

Phrygian Stone Idol from the Southeast Gate of Büyükkale:
MDOG No. 93 (1962), pp. 47f.

Stone Idol from Fahared Çeşme near Ankara:
Von der Osten, H. H. *Explorations in Central Anatolia, Season of 1926* (Oriental Institute Publications, Vol. V, Chicago, 1929 p. 59 with fig. 90 and plate V B.)

Monument (Altar) of the So-called Midas City:

Bossert, H. Th. *Altanatolien* (Berlin, 1942), No. 1101, pp. 289.

Gabriel, Albert. *Phrygie IV. La Cité de Midas, Architecture* (Paris, 1965). p. 45, fig. 26, and plate 20 a, b, d.

High Circular Platform below Büyükkale:

MDOG No. 88 (1955), pp. 12ff. with illustrations.

INDEX

Abu Simbel, 127, 128
Adana, 114
Akurgal, Ekrem, 137, 168
Alaca Hüyük, 80, 107, 114, 136, 147
Aleppo, 118, 121
Alişar, 19, 45, 46, 49, 49, 133, 138
Allen, T. George, 165
Amarna, 8, 113
Amenhotep III, 8, 121
Amenhotep IV (Akhenaten), 8, 121, 122
Amurru, 124
Andrae, Walter, 107
Ankara, 140, 150, 152
Anitta, 18, 19, 47
Arık, Remzi Oğuz, 165
Arinna, Sun Goddess of, 6, 49, 57
Arnuwanda, 51
Arslankaya, 152, 153
Arzawa, 8, 9
Assyria, 133, 135, 136

Babylon, 125
Balıkkaya, 28
Balkan, Kemal, 45, 162
Barnett, R. D., 167
Barth, H., 92
Beran, Thomas, 160, 163, 168
Bitik, 100
Bossert, E.-M., 169
Bossert, H. Th., 169
Breasted, James B., 166
Byblos, 114, 119, 120

Çalapverdi, 133
Carchemish, 90, 120, 121, 122, 131, 134, 135, 136
Chantre, Ernest, 8, 159
Christian, Victor, 93
Cilicia, 135, 155
Cıradere, 28
Croesus, 7, 155, 156
Cyrus, 155, 156

Dattashsha, 20, 21, 22, 88, 123
Diyarbakır, 109

Edel, Elmar, 166, 167

Fahared Çeşme, 152
Fischer, Franz, 162
Frankfort, Henri, 161
Friedrich, J., 168

Gabriel, A., 169
Garelli, P., 44, 46, 162
Goetze, Albrecht, 161, 162, 163
Gordion, 136, 140, 142, 144, 152
Gurney, O. R., 161
Güterbock, H. G., 110, 160, 163, 164, 165, 166

Haas, Otto, 168
Hamilton, W. J., 92
Hantili, 20, 48, 120
Hattushili I, 3, 6, 19, 20, 47, 49, 118, 120
Hattushili III, 9, 15, 20, 21, 60, 66, 88, 103, 113, 119, 124, 125, 126, 127, 129
Helck, W., 117, 163, 165, 166
Hepat, 94, 96, 97, 98, 99
Herodotus, 7, 136, 155, 156
Horemheb, 123
Houwink ten Cate, P. H. J., 167
Humann, Carl, 10, 13
Hyksos, 116, 117, 118, 120

Imamkulu, 98, 100
Inandık, 100
Ini-Teshub, 90

Jacob-Rost, Liane, 162

Kanesh, 17, 18, 19, 33, 34, 44, 45, 46
Kārum Hattush, 18, 43, 47, 48
Kārum Kanesh, 44, 45, 46, 115
Kashka, 11, 20, 21, 88, 90, 134, 135, 155
Kashku, 133, 134, 139
Khyan, 116, 117, 118, 120
Kimmerian invasion, 136, 142
Kırıkkale, 114, 115
Knossos, 117
Körte, G. and A., 167
Koşay, Hâmit Z., 165
Krause, Karl, 162
Kubaba (Kybele), 134, 150, 151, 152, 153
Kuentz, C., 166
Kültepe (Kanesh), 17, 18, 19, 33, 44, 45, 115
Kummanni, 21
Kushshar, 18, 19, 47

Landsberger, Benno, 107, 167
Laroche, Emmanuel, 94, 97, 99, 104, 160, 161, 164, 168
Lewy, Hildegard, 161
Luckenbill, D. D., 167

Makridi, Theodore, 9
Mari, 19, 119
Mellink, Machteld J., 167
Merenptah, 90, 130
MESHEDI-text, 64, 65, 66, 74, 86
Meyer, Eduard, 92
Mezulla, 6, 49
Midas (Mita), 135, 136, 137, 142
Midas City, 149, 150, 152
Mitanni, 120, 121
Murshili I, 20, 118, 120
Murshili II, 64, 134
Murshili III (Urhi-Teshub), 22, 88, 103, 125
Mushki, 133, 134, 135, 136, 137
Muwatalli, 20, 21, 22, 88, 102, 123, 124, 125, 127

Naram-Sin, 17, 18, 35
Naster, P., 167
Naumann, Rudolf, 82, 160, 161, 164
Nergal, 110
Nesha, 19, 47
Neve, P., 161, 162, 168

Orthmann, W., 161
Otten, Heinrich, 45, 107, 109, 110, 161, 162, 163, 164
Özgüç, Tahsin, 164

Pamba, 17, 18, 35
Pijushti, 19, 47
Pritchard, James B., 165, 166
Pteria, 7, 91, 155, 156
Puchstein, Otto, 10, 160
Puduhepa, 15, 126, 128

Qadesh, 124, 125
Qatna, 119

Ramesses II, 9, 15, 88, 103, 113, 119, 123, 124, 125, 126, 127, 128, 129, 130
Ramesses III, 131
Ras Shamra, *see* Ugarit
Ruge, W., 167

Sargon of Akkad, 17
Sargon II, 133, 136, 155
Sayce, A. H., 8, 159
Schaeffer, C. F.-A., 164
Schäffer, E., 8, 159
Schirmer, W., 161
Schmökel, H., 161
Schuler, Einar von, 166
Shamshi-Adad I, 45
Sharruma, 96, 98, 99, 101, 102, 127
Shaushga, 96
Sheri and Hurri, 72, 73, 98, 99, 100
Shuppiluliuma I, 8, 20, 60, 66, 113, 118, 121, 122, 123
Shuppiluliuma II, 60, 90, 110, 111, 133
Sinope, 156
Smith, W. Stevenson, 155, 165
Sterrett, J. R. Sitlington, 7, 159
Stock, Hanns, 165

Tabal, 133, 134, 135, 137, 150, 155
Talmi-Teshub, 90
Tarsus, 107
Tavium, 7
Teshub, 96, 97, 98, 99
Texier, Charles, 7, 91, 93, 159
Tiglath-Pileser I, 135, 136
Tiglath-Pileser III, 133, 136
Tukulti-Ninurta I, 90

Tutankhamen, 122
Tuthaliya, 102, 104, 110, 111
Tuthaliya III, 20, 49, 96, 111, 121
Tuthaliya IV, 16, 66, 85, 89, 90, 96, 101, 103, 104, 123, 127, 132
Tuthmosis III, 120, 121
Tyana, 136, 137

Ugarit (Ras Shamra), 102, 103, 114, 119, 120
Urartu, 133, 135, 136
Urhi-Teshub (Murshili III), 22, 88, 125

Vergote, J., 166
Von der Osten, H. H., 165, 168

Weather God of Hatti, 49, 57, 94, 96
Winckler, Hugo, 7, 8, 9, 10, 113, 122, 160
Wright, W., 8, 159

Young, Rodney S., 167

Zimmern, H., 107

PLATES

Akkadian text of King Hattushili I. H. *ca.* 0.28 m

a. Boğazköy, view from north

b. Boğazköy, model of city area seen from east

PLATE 2

a. Boğazköy, view from northeast

b. Building K on Büyükkale, archive room with tablets on bench

a. Levels on west side of Büyükkale

b. Levels in southwest part of Büyükkale

PLATE 4

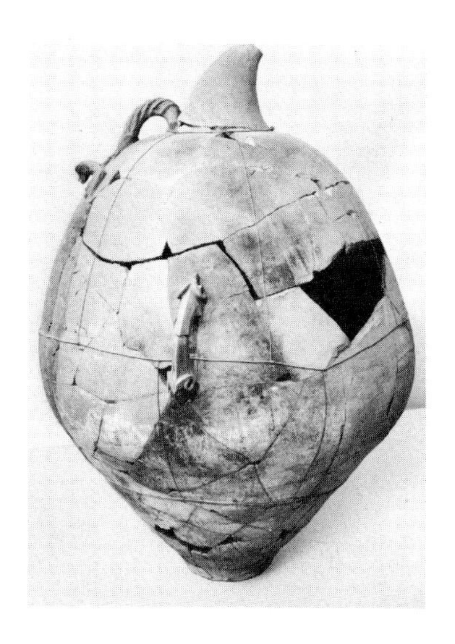
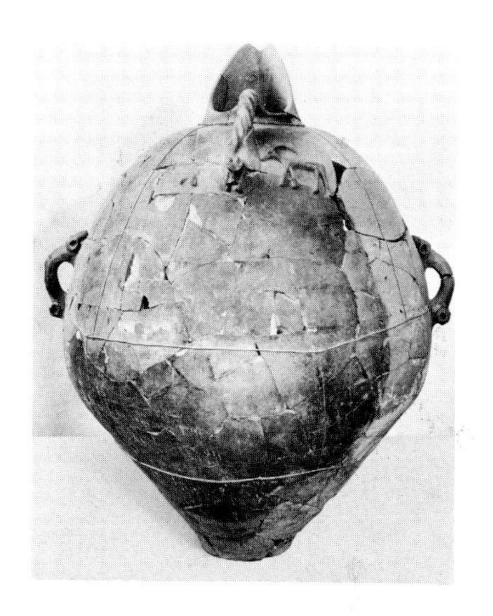

Storage pitcher from Büyükkale. H. 1.35 m

a. House in the kārum Hattush

b. Old Assyrian clay tablets

PLATE 6

Stamp-seals and cylinder seal from the kārum Hattush. H. 0.025-0.031 m

PLATE 7

a. Lead figurine of god from kārum Hattush. H. 0.074 m

b. Casting mould for figurine of Potnia Therôn, kārum Hattush, with cast. H. 0.078 m

Lion-shaped vessels from Büyükkale. L. *ca.* 0.22 m

PLATE 9

a. Beaked pitcher from the kārum Hattush. H. 0.384 m

b. Vase fragment with tower and crenellations. Maximum preserved height 0.12 m

PLATE 10

a. Tunnel of postern at Yerkapı

b. Yerkapı seen from south

a. Lion gate, view of exterior

b. Royal gate, seen from interior of city

c. Royal gate, seen from exterior

PLATE 12

a. Temples II-III from south

b. Temple I, view from east

a. Inscription on Nişantaş. H. of lines *ca.* 0.35 m

b. Büyükkale from south

a. Bull-shaped vessels from Büyükkale as found

b. The vessels as restored. H. 0.91 m

a. Bull-vase seen from above

b. Bull-vase seen in profile

PLATE 16

a. North side of Büyükkale, wall and tower near top of cliff

b. Yazılıkaya from south

Yazılıkaya, procession of gods

PLATE 18

a. Mountain gods supporting main god

b. Ivory statuette of Mountain God.
H. 0.0368 m

a. Yazılıkaya, main god and goddess

b. Yazılıkaya, main scene. H. of smoothed rock-surface *ca*. 2.60 m

a. Yazılıkaya, relief of Tuthaliya, main chamber. H. of smoothed rock-surface 2.95 m

b. Yazılıkaya, Sun and Moon gods. H. 0.85 m and 0.81 m

Yazılıkaya, bull-men supporting sky. H. of smoothed rock-surface *ca.* 1.00 m

Yazılıkaya, lion-headed demons at entrance to side-chamber. H. *ca.* 1.00 m

a. Yazılıkaya, side chamber, east wall

b. Yazılıkaya, group of twelve gods. H. of smoothed rock-surface *ca.* 0.82 m

a. Yazılıkaya, relief of Sharruma and Tuthaliya (cast). H. *ca.* 1.67 m

b. Yazılıkaya, Sword God. H. 3.39 m

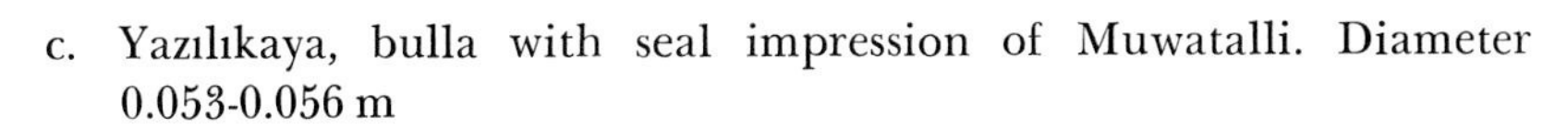

c. Yazılıkaya, bulla with seal impression of Muwatalli. Diameter 0.053-0.056 m

b. Phrygian ivory seal.
H. 0.016 m

a. Abu Simbel. Relief showing Hattushili III and his daughter

c. Relief from Nineveh: capture of the city of Hamanu

a. Phrygian house, Büyükkale level II

b. Phrygian glacis and paved street on west side of Büyükkale

a. Phrygian staircase on west slope of Büyükkale

b. Phrygian well-shaft, west slope of Büyükkale

PLATE 28

Group statue of Kybele-Kubaba and attendants. H. including base 1.34 m

PLATE 29

Round structure at south side of Büyükkale

PLATE 30